Unificationist Home Groups Manual

Unificationist Home Groups Manual:

For the Success of Home Groups, One-to-One Teaching, Oikos (Home Church) and Vision 2020

Translated and Edited by Trevor Davies

From the 2015 Spanish and Portuguese versions by Koichi Sasaki

Cover Design by Toby Suda

Published by PureLiving Media Ltd. 2017

First English Language Printing: 2017

ISBN 978-0-244-02597-7

PureLiving Media Ltd.
165 Restons Crescent
London SE9 2JH

www.purelivingmedia.com

admin@purelivingmedia.com

Ordering Information:

Please contact the publisher at the above listed address or email
admin@purelivingmedia.com

Contents

Acknowledgements

I would like to thank Pres. Koichi Sasaki (National Leader FFWPU Brazil) for permission to translate and publish this book in English.

Thanks to Matthew and Natasha Huish (FFWPU U.K. National Leaders) for giving me the opportunity to develop the Home Groups providence in our local community which led to my discovering and translating this manual. I am grateful for their encouragement and patience.

Thank you to the several people who helped with proofreading, Ron Chandler, Ollie Davies, David Hanna, Edward Hartley, Joy Philippou and Daniel Pollitt.

Finally thank you to Toby Suda for designing the cover and to Ollie Davies for designing the accompanying PowerPoint slides.

Preface

The idea of Home Groups or Small Groups or Cell Groups is not new. For several decades various Home Group methods have been used to grow churches and other organisations all over the world. There are several mega churches having profound impact in their local areas and beyond because they have been able to grow successfully into large, prosperous and effective faith-based organisations.

Home/Small Groups are also not new to Unificationists. Many of our activities have been and are done in teams – small groups - and we have all been aware of mega churches growing around the world for several decades. Those mega churches have all used Small Groups or Home Group Ministries as a method of church growth often combined with a very well planned and delivered Sunday Service ministry. Many books have been written on the subject, the most appealing and successful are founded on solid Biblical Principles. But as a Unificationist looking for a model to base our own church growth on, I found all of those books to be deficient in some way.

This manual however is something very special. It is the result of more than a decade of pioneering work by Unificationists in Brazil and other countries in South America and explains in detail how to develop a Home Groups ministry and grow the church with new members, not only based on Biblical and sound psychological principles but primarily based on the application of Divine Principle. The Home Groups described in this manual are not only for the education of existing members or to provide a place to meet socially but are to facilitate exponential growth in membership that is both feasible and manageable.

In Brazil they have experienced a "witnessing explosion". Details of this impressive growth of the FFWPU in South American can easily be found online, though most of the content is in Portuguese or Spanish. If we want FFWPU to grow in the UK or in Europe or other parts of the world, a good place to start would be to adopt a method that has already proven to be successful.

A word of caution though! It is very easy to think that methods employed on other continents will work over there but not here – we might say because of social, religious or historical differences. It is also tempting to think that you can take part of a system and use just that small part, or to change and adapt it to "local circumstances" but beware – this is an integrated system that works as it is. If you feel to change any of it, do so wisely and consider whether your changes are sustainable and easily duplicated. And don't do so until you have a thorough understanding of why this system is successful as it is.

I am not the author of the original Unificationist Home Groups Manual, Koichi Sasaki in Brazil wrote the original text which I translated and edited. This is the first English translation of the updated Spanish translation of the Portuguese Home Groups Manual.

I have endeavoured to be true to the original text but it may still be evident that this is a translation. However, as an English first edition it is sufficient to start a witnessing revolution in Europe if enough people can be moved by the spirit of God to embrace the content and develop Home Groups in their local communities and start to grow our church like never before. It will be very difficult for an isolated group to achieve this on their own but if a significant number of people work together and cooperate to develop this ministry in their local church community and share mutual support internationally, then I am convinced that we too can experience the kind of church growth that we all crave.

It is with this purpose in mind that I am developing an online community of Unificationist Homegroups to share experience, best practice and educational resources. One of the challenges I experienced as a Group Host was to find suitable material for study and discussion. So I have started to create a number of study series based on the content of *World Scripture 2 and the Teachings of Sun Myung Moon*. This will be available very soon for download on the publisher's website and I hope that others will feel inspired to share their resources through the same site.

Translating and publishing this manual has been a kind of Noah's Ark for me – but I'm sure that even that magnificent vessel had a few leaks, it lacked elegance but it served its purpose in allowing Mankind to make a new start.

Trevor Davies – Bromley, London – U.K. – August 2017

Contact: trevor@pureliving.co.uk

Introduction

Rev. Dong Mo Shin

Why did we make Home Groups? – a church that can resurrect the nation through two wings

With the victory of Foundation Day through True Parents, the substantial Cheon Il Guk began. We participated in the Holy Wine Ceremony on the Foundation Day of Cheon Il Guk owing to the sacrifices and sufferings throughout the life course of True Parents and we received such great love. We received the mandate of Heaven to expand from now on, on Earth, the substantial Cheon Il Guk initiated by the victorious True Parents. After True Father's Seong-Hwa (ascension), True Mother proclaimed that we would make determined progress without interruption and asked for all members to invest all their efforts into witnessing, in order to fulfil the mission of tribal messiah.

Then, how are we going to do this? What should our church be like in the Era of Cheon Il Guk? We need to engage with this issue. On the foundation of all the accomplishments of the previous era, the era of indemnity, we need to make a new beginning, following only the tradition and the lineage that True Parents have established, with a firm resolution to be more conformed to them. Thus, we must become "*The true owners of Cheon Il Guk that practice True Love in the likeness of our Creator, the Heavenly Parents*", which was given as the motto for our life up to 2020.

Today we mark the important start for the salvation of all humanity on the basis of searching for the true self - "I" and the true family through the vision of Home Groups, One-to-one Tuition and Oikos (Home Church).

Just before the time of his 'Soeng-Hwa" (ascension), True Father said that fulfilling our "Tribal Messiah" mission is the first priority of our lives. 2000 years ago, for Jesus it was the same. In Matthew 28 are recorded the last words of Jesus. The main content of these words, transmitted to the disciples was to go out to society and make more disciples with the confidence that they could bring a change to society. This was the vision of Jesus.

True Father gave these words, *"I am old now, and so for how many more years will I be able to witness? How many people up to the time of my death? How many thousands or tens of thousands of people can I testify to? This is what I am always thinking. By doing so, establishing a plan, thinking about how many thousand persons of this kind exist, how long will it take to restore the 5 billion people of humanity? Even those people that still do not understand the truth, our descendants, generations and generations, we have to free all the people with the ideology of fire. For this reason, the tribe to whom I can leave this type of last word is one that can inherit the Heavenly Nation."*

(True Parents and the Renaissance Vol. 251, P. 204, 10.17.1993)

We who are living in this significant time, we received the last words of True Parents. Recalling these words and teachings, and thinking of the words that Jesus spoke 2000 years ago, we have to understand clearly the meaning of our church and the vision of Home Groups. Establishing blessed couples as representatives of True Parents in our church, giving life to the Nation, reaching the level of the Continent, we will save the 7 billion people of humanity.

What shall we do to achieve this? This is the vision of the development of "two wings", the large group and small group of our church. Completely developing the existing church and at the same time, causing an explosion of Home Groups, which are small church communities, we will make the dream of Heaven in this era. This is our small repayment to True Parents who gave us the entire realm of victory almost for free through the Holy Wine Ceremony and Blessing of Foundation Day.

Don't say come, instead, go

Thinking about how our Church operates, we always want people to come to us to receive words of truth. This is not a wrong desire, but it seems to me different from the desire of True Parents and the purpose that they gave to the churches. The church is at the centre of the culture of heart (shimjong) and is an education organization. We have to manage the church with these functions. No one can deny the need for the church building. We need a building with the purpose of gathering everyone together to hear sermons, gather to communicate and gather to be trained.

The main purpose of the existence of the church itself is to witness. In other words, we can conclude that the purpose of the church is to bear witness to people who do not know about God and True Parents and to transform them into good children of God and True Parents, believing in God and receiving the Holy Blessing. The Church body does not say "come to us", but rather "we go to you" to people at witnessing time. Consider how few people seek a church when they feel depressed. How about those who are not looking for a church, will they have to go to hell too? We have to go to families, to villages, to places of work, to the locations where those people live. This is witnessing centring on relationships. This is "Oikos (Home Church)", where we use words naturally in the normal relationships of our daily life.

Academics have stated that until now there is the "gathered church" and the "scattered church". Before we began Home Group activities, when we were talking about the growth of the church, we only emphasised the "gathered church ". We are looking for great change in these coming years, meeting new challenges. For members in Brazil, words such as "Home Groups, One-to-one and Oikos (Home Church)" are not unfamiliar words any more. With this point of view, the fact that you don't have a bright building for the church is not a disastrous thing that prevents the church from growing. In fact, a fundamental issue is that we, as people of faith, have to emphasize our personality, conjugal relationships, family and healthy community. Also another key issue is in what manner we are living. We are families who were born through True Parents. We have been pretending that we are people of faith, going to the Sunday Service, but in practice, in reality, we have been living a life that has nothing to do with faith. From now on, we have to go out to society. If it is true that our life changed completely through the Blessing and salvation of True Parents, this same value can change this society which is divided into mediocrity. This is the reason why we are making family churches, in the family and in the workplace. To implement a Home Group, there is no immediate need to have a building. We just need a space where we can gather some people, where there are words of Hoon Dok Hae, where heart and love for one another can be shared, and we can share personal problems (and as couples of course.) In a place where you can share the effort that each person makes, life is happier, where it is possible to feel one another's suffering, strengthen the weak points of another and to love people that are difficult to love, life is happier. In this way, the Home Group must be a place that has an atmosphere of love. In this place, although it is not so bright externally, if I have heart and love, the people that meet there, can experience Cheon Il Guk.

This is the reason why our church (in Brazil) considers the Home Group vision as the most important purpose of all. More than constructing a building, we have to give importance to each one of us practicing and sharing heart and true love centred on the words of True Parents, looking for people in society. To repeat, now we can no longer be that kind of "Sunday Member" who only participates in the Sunday Service at church, but we have to be "every day" members, who on a daily basis practice a life of substantial word and substantial faith.

We have to educate directly with the Divine Principle book.

True Parents said that those who were first to hear the Divine Principle have to teach it to others. True Parents taught us in detail that only with the book, we can give a lecture. Even though we are not a professional lecturer, we can teach the Divine Principle with the book. For this reason, in the beginning of the 1990s, colours were used to allow us to vary the duration of reading times. True Parents gave special instructions that everyone should give One-to-one lectures. Already (in Brazil), many members have practiced this and feel major changes and grace directly. To witness does not only mean to guide others to have life, but also to bring a change for oneself and get excited about it. We can experience this.

True Parents guide us that we must teach the Divine Principle from start to finish and not just a part of it. Although we have only one hour at a time, we have to explain the Divine Principle from the introduction until the end without omitting any part. That is why the Divine Principle appeared with three colours. Through many experiences, we know that reading and explaining only the red and blue parts is sufficient to understand the Divine Principle and it takes about 30 hours to complete. Thus, to give spiritual life, we teach the Divine Principle directly for several hours together with conditions of devotion and love.

In reality, it is not so easy to educate through One-to-one tuition. However, through practice, we may feel great emotion and grace. We can be spiritually resurrected. Through the Principle, we can understand the purpose of creation, human responsibility and the providence of restoration. The guests will understand naturally that only through the sacred marriage of True Parents is possible to become God's children again, by eliminating the root of sin. In this way, only through the Divine Principle, can fallen people understand the way of salvation and deliverance to become citizens of Heaven.

Through the Home Groups, we can live together with true love and teach people to undertake what we teach them straightaway

We still have a long way to go, even though we have already learned the Divine Principle and we started to practice a life of faith. We need to prepare for the Blessing and later, to live life as a Blessed Family after the Blessing ceremony. Our life of faith does not end when we receive the Blessing. The Blessing, strictly speaking, is the true starting point and new beginning.

For Blessed Families to perform their original role we teach the lessons that True Parents gave us and we guide them to fulfil them. Equally since we need to study for the continued growth of our spiritual selves on Earth, this study would be necessary in schools. But the most important place in life where this study should be conducted is in the family, where we experience and embody the love and heart of Heaven through the relationship of spouses, brothers and sisters and parents and children. Home Group activities are more like an extended family. The Home Group teaching is practice in real life on the premise of compliance and obedience to the words. This type of teaching does not work without an example to be followed. In the family, children do not learn what parents tell them; rather they learn through the actions of the parents. Similarly, when a person believes in True Parents, is it possible to teach them to live as Unificationists? Those new members learn by watching how others live.

It might be possible to do this in the main church where we meet once a week, on Sundays. But in the midst of many people, without knowing anyone more deeply, how can the guest learn by watching us? That is why you need the Home Group, that is, a small *cell group*. What if that were a place where a community is formed by the members of the group, surely it would possible to become an example to each guest personally? This is the vision of Home Groups that Heaven gave us, a strategy of Heaven in the Era of Cheon Il Guk, a method to educate and create citizens of Cheon Il Guk.

Jesus called the 12 apostles and lived together with them. Of course he testified, and demonstrated his teachings. That is why the apostles could easily learn by watching his actions. True Parents, when they had the opportunity, would call the National Messiahs and leaders and had activities together, passing traditions onto them.

True Parents, just like Jesus 2000 years ago, had many discussions with their disciples, but in truth, the essence of their mission was training for the disciples. True Parents took the main disciples to the interior of South America and to Alaska, spent many nights with them, suffering, practicing and teaching the disciples eternal truths.

The disciples learned from True Father that they should create other disciples, who in turn would create and mobilize other new disciples. When we have such a vision, there will be many people in this world who will live in accordance with his teaching. He believed that this was the only hope for this world. True Parents, having this standard, asked with all their heart that we all accomplish the mission of Tribal Messiah. True Father emphasized that we should give priority to witnessing more than anything else, to save all 7 billion people of humanity.

We in the church (in Brazil), are going to expand Cheon Il Guk through Oikos (Home Church), taking the vision of Home Groups and One-to-one tuition as a tool. We have this dream and hope.

Although we meet many people, we cannot hope for a fundamental change in this world by dealing with the masses. They are nothing more than observers. I don't want our church to only increase the number of observers.

Then, having become a big family, how can we grow up not as observers, but as people who have a role? In our church, we provide many words and many of us speak on the Principle, but we cannot change the world through this. So how can we do it? Our response is unique. All of us members, entering into a structure of the extended family and sharing an honest life, need to go to the positions where we received training as a representative of True Parents. This is the Home Group.

People set weekly and monthly targets through which they substantiate the words, sharing the contents and words through practicing them. In this way, we need to create a community in the church where there are hopes and dreams. That community can take the many people suffering from the problems of this era such as family breakdown, teenage immorality, depression etc. and be able to rejuvenate their original minds, going beyond the district, nation, and continent and to the world.

Beloved leaders and family members!

True Father said the following words:

"What is my only concern? Among you, after my death, how many people can love the members of the Unification Church centred on the heart of love for God? If we cannot love with all our love, with such love that longs so much to love God, facing death, how many people will mourn in sobs of tears? If you all were like that, when I die, although you bury me in any way you like, I will not remain resentful".

(Sermons of Rev. Sun Myung Moon Volume 22 p. 107. 1969.01.26)

Beloved family members! I hope that all members of the Church in this nation and throughout the continent, without any exception, will form a Home Group, even if it is small, but with a big vision, and become Home Group leaders and practice teaching directly through One-to-one tuition. Share true love; make intimate relationships with those closest to you, as members of the same Home Group. Then devote yourselves especially to those small things. I shed tears of emotion every time that there is a multiplying of Home Group cells through their practice of true love and "jeongsong".

True love, even when it is small, has a lot of strength. It can transform death into life. And also, it possesses an almost magical force through which you can naturally subdue enemies. We are still small, but we have a great vision for Home Groups. Now, all of us together we are going to move forward and reach our victory.

Although a match is a small thing, it can burn an entire field. In this Home Group Manual, we have gathered and organized all the knowledge that we gained through the experiences of our activities, and also the contents of visioneering seminars.

I believe that, through this material, all of you can study and learn in more detail the contents that you already heard in the *Vision of Home Groups* seminars.

Read this book line by line with jeongsong (sincere dedication), memorize exactly the meaning and intentions and confirm the contents between yourselves. When you understand it clearly, by starting and practicing the contents and establishing ideal Home Groups, then an explosive feeling can occur. I hope that you, in this way, invest your jeongsong to firmly understand this purpose. I thank all those who devoted themselves to create this manual investing their jeongsong, centred on the president. I believe that this manual will become good and essential material for the Home Group Movement that can save the Nation and the Continent. I pray for great blessings and love of the Heavenly Parents and True Parents of Heaven, Earth and Mankind.

São Paulo

Continental President of Latin America and special Cheon Il Guk Envoy of Brazil

Rev. Dong Mo Shin

Chapter 1.
Internal Guidance

The reason why we have internal guidance in the first part of this book is because we have used content from the Divine Principle as a basis for Home Group activities. We haven't created the Home Group system based only on Christian ideas or from popular psychology but based it on the Divine Principle.

When we read Divine Principle in detail, word by word, line by line, we can understand that it is the best internal guide and solves many uncertainties of life. First, we developed internal guidance based on the Divine Principle and from this internal guidance we have extracted the core content for our Home Groups system. For a long time, not only Christians, but also the communists and other organizations have been doing something similar through family homes in many countries. But there is a great difference between them and our Home Group activities. We have the Divine Principle that they do not have.

If someone loses patience and tries to learn about Home Groups without first understanding this internal guidance, their understanding becomes superficial and without a basis to understand the true purpose of each aspect of Home Groups. We use the Divine Principle in the Home Groups, which is why Home Groups is an activity that can bring us to individual perfection and unity within couples, thus accomplishing the Three Great Blessings on earth and fulfilling our Purpose of Creation. We believe that the victorious "national explosion" of witnessing success also depends very much on understanding and practicing Divine Principle in the Home Groups.

Individual Perfection, Unity within Couples and Home Groups

The First Blessing

To complete "Individual Perfection" is our goal in life. Beyond being the goal of a life of faith, it is also the goal of our whole lives. This is not only the goal of the members of our church, but also the goal of every human being.

The Divine Principle defines the First Blessing in the following way: In order for an individual to perfect his or her character, they must form a four position foundation within themselves whereby the mind and body become one through give and take action with God as their centre.

The Divine Principle continues to explain the value of the perfect person:

1. *The perfected man becomes the temple of God,*
2. *forms one body with God,*
3. *reaches his/her divinity,*
4. *feels exactly what God feels,*
5. *knows the will of God and*
6. *lives exactly as God wants him to live.*

Becoming the Temple of God means to become the body of God or God's image. Reaching divinity means incorporating the nature of God, this is the opposite of having fallen nature. We must have all the qualities that God has and not have those qualities that God does not have. If a person is able to feel everything that God feels they become one body with God. Then they can't do anything against the will of God, since the mind of God will be their mind.

For a long time, human beings have striven for the betterment of society through politics, education, etc., but those solutions only resolved problems superficially. However, if each one of us comes to feel exactly what God feels, this will be the best way to resolve all the fundamental problems from the root. When every human has this point of view, it will be a world where it would be impossible to injure each other. For example, it would prevent war from starting because such a person would feel the pain of God directly because of such a war.

In accordance with the Principle, the perfect person:

7. *Immediately feels everything that God feels, as if God's feelings were their own.*
8. *Such a person does not do anything that causes suffering to God,*
9. *Therefore can never commit sin or fall.*

This is the goal of the life of faith. Independent of the activities in which a person is involved (for example distributing autobiographies, mobilization for events, testimonials, Home Groups, etc.), the common aim is individual perfection through such activities. Eventually, a person will have to reach that standard, the standard of individual perfection presented in the Divine Principle.

What activities do we do in a life of faith? Sometimes we worry a lot about the external aspect of providential activities. On the other hand, the innermost part may sometimes be forgotten and that is how to achieve the standard of perfection through the victory of love. The mastery of the internal aspect is more essential and subject to the external aspect of the life of faith.

While we strive for the Kingdom of Heaven, and are developing true love, we will be able to perceive that we are lacking internal conditions to live in the Kingdom of heaven. The "external activity" and "individual perfection" are like two gears. If one gear becomes disconnected from the other, although one of them is running well, the other will stop. Only when they are connected will the movement of one give movement to the other. In the same way, we must not disconnect in our minds the concepts of "external activity" and "individual perfection". Through performing external activities, we must pursue our individual perfection. We must find our individual perfection through the external activities.

In general, there is a tendency to place "external activities" in the position of subject, and forget the other side, the more internal activities. However the right thing to do is place "individual perfection" in the position of subject and the "external activity" in the object position. If church members forget this important point, fights between them may occur because of different views on "what is the correct way to perform such and such activity". But if each one reminds the other that their common goal is become a temple of God, to form one body with God and grow in true love, then they will not fight. Once they clearly understand these standards of individual perfection, they will become more modest and will lose the desire to criticize others. It is vitally important not to forget that those 9 individual standards of perfection are the ultimate goals of our lives.

God does not want to be away from human beings, he wants to be within them. God wants to love and govern all things through mankind and walk on the Earth, "wearing" their body. The more a person comes closer to the union of the mind and the body, the more God and Man will come closer. If we complete the unity of mind and body, we will be completing the union between God and Man as well. The relationship between God and Man is the same as the relationship between the mind and body. The body acts naturally in accordance with the will of the mind. In the case of the perfect person, the same thoughts of God would be their thoughts and without time delay, the person would already be doing what God wants. In this way it would be impossible for that person to hurt God because they would feel the same pain as God.

The ideal world is the world where it is impossible to commit sin. No need for religion, laws, judges or punishment. Once we perfectly feel the heart of God, we also feel the heart of one another, because God has the heart of all. It becomes impossible to mistreat each other.

Certainly, formal education and social activities are very important for the improvement of society, but without understanding the Divine Principle, you will have limited ability to solve all the problems. The Divine Principle explains starting from the most essential truths and presents the most complete and perfect solution. This is the key to finding the solutions to the problems of the individual, marital problems and all other problems in general.

In our life of faith, performing the 1st blessing is the main focus for any activity. We call it a blessing because it generates joy. When we do this, the heavenly joy of God arises in us as a source and continues infinitely. In the ideal world, ideal people do not need to endeavour and suffer for love, because love will flow naturally from one to the other. Happiness begins within each one of us and does not depend on external circumstances or how we are treated by each other.

The way to unify the mind and the body not only depends on discipline, (denying the desires of the body), but also depends on the stimulation of the love of God. First the mind must be completely united with God and receiving love from Him. This mind acquires enough force to dominate the body. For this purpose, the mind should not have fallen nature and sin, but must have love whose nature is equal to God. Fallen nature is what prevents the love of God from flowing into us. Sin is what separates in the relationship between God and us. If we do not have true love, we don't have resonance with God. That is why we are sometimes unable to receive the strong stimulation of the love of God to dominate the desires of the flesh.

We are going to reflect once again on those 9 qualities of individual perfection. If we do not accomplish these, we cannot call it "individual perfection". As soon as we have any fallen nature, we cannot be the temple of God and if we have sins, we cannot form one body with Him. If we do not have true love, we don't reach divinity.

We are fallen people, and that is why we are locked out from the love of God, but in the original world we will of course grow into the unity of mind and body centred on the love of God.

In the life of faith, sometimes spiritual phenomenon can happen and we feel wonderfully good. But that is not the essence of individual perfection. In the Divine Principle, spiritual events are not criteria for the standard of individual perfection.

Then in what way must we improve ourselves? The essence of an individual's perfection is a matter of the maturity of love. Individual perfection is the perfection of love. Jesus showed the pattern of perfection that we each need to reach:

"At that time, Jesus said to his disciples: "You heard what was said: You shall love your neighbour and hate your enemy! I, however I can tell you: Love your enemies and pray for those who persecute you! Well, you will again be sons of your Father who is in Heaven, because he makes the sun rise on the evil and the good and the rain to fall on the just and the unjust. Because, what if you love only those who love you, what reward is that? Don't even the tax collectors do the same? And if you greet only your brothers, what are you doing that is special? Do not even the pagans do the same? Therefore, "Be perfect as your Father who is in heaven is perfect"

(Matthew 5:43-48).

Jesus said that, what we need to refine, is nothing other than our love.

If we fail to grow in our love through our activities, we are not living a life of faith in a correct manner. If our growth of love stops, even though we are doing many things externally and even making results, we can be deceived, because we are not reaching the most fundamental goal which is internal growth through passing the "Formula Course" and achieving the perfection of love. You can even experience the opposite, for example, increasing arrogance because of your results or create resentment because of your sacrifice. If that happens in our life we will only have achievements from "activities", without passing the "Formula Course". We must not mentally detach "external activities" from "Formula Course". If we are not clear about what constitutes the standard of individual perfection, we can't be very clear about the differences between "activities" and completing the "Formula Course". As a result, the purpose of our life of faith becomes empty.

In conclusion - why do we do Home Group activities? So each person can successfully complete the "Formula Course" and achieve the perfection of love.

The Second Blessing

The Divine Principle explains that for person to accomplish the 2nd blessing, Adam and Eve, as the divided dual characteristics of God and substantial objects that have perfected their individuality, must become a couple and should form a family base of four positions centred on God, by multiplying their children through the connection between them.

Within the explanation of a couple three important points are made and the value of Mankind and the universe appears. The first point is that Man is the substantial, total incorporation of the macrocosm with man as the subject partner and the woman as an object partner. When the two make a perfect couple they are able to represent the entire universe.

The second point is that Man is the master of the macrocosm. The mind of Man dominates the subject part of the spiritual universe and the body of Man dominates the subject part of the physical universe. Woman dominates his mind with the object part of the spiritual universe and the body with the object part of the physical universe. That way through the per-perfect union of the couple they can dominate the entire creation. Then the union of the couple is the centre of the entire dominion of the creation. The third point explains that man is the centre of harmony of the whole macrocosm. Through the unity of mind and body of a perfect couple there is harmony between the physical world and the spiritual world. The union of a perfect couple becomes the centre of harmony of the entire macrocosm.

The purpose of creation is realised when God, the subject of love, and a person, the object of beauty, become a single unit; the point of unity of a perfected couple, is the centre of the goodness. Goodness means something that carries out the purpose of God. God can feel great joy when human beings achieve the ideal of a perfected couple (true parents) which is the full realization of the dream of God from the beginning of the creation. That is why the Divine Principle shows that at this time, for the first time, God (True Parents) can dwell with perfected people (their children) and remain peacefully for all eternity. Thus, the centre of unity of the perfected couple becomes the object of the eternal love of God and through this God will feel joy for all eternity.

Then, what is the way to free God and allow Him to feel joy for all eternity? To accomplish that, each of us must become part of a perfected couple of individually harmonious individuals. Then we will be able to experience the true love of God. When a couple achieves this, the Word of God will be incarnated substantially for the first time. The point of unity for the couple will be the centre of truth and the mind that directs all original human beings to achieve the purpose of creation. Here a person experiences the total liberation of the mind and lives only by the stimulation of the original mind. No evil mind remains in a person when they are 100% filled with the love of God. A couple can express the whole principle of the creation in a substantial way, without using the book, simply through their daily life. Whoever sees a perfect couple looks at all of the attributes of God substantiated in them. Within that partnership there is the whole truth of the universe. The perfect couple has that type of value.

True Father's speech *"The Providential View of History of Salvation" explains this matter:*

"But God as the subject of True Love did establish humankind as the object of His True Love. Accordingly, God can fulfil His ideal of True Love only through humankind. The fulfilment of God's Purpose of Creation is the ideal world where God and mankind are united through absolute love. Human beings were created as the greatest object of God's love. They alone in all Creation embody the nature of God. They are born the visible bodies of the invisible God. If a person perfects himself, he becomes the temple of God, a visible, substantial body in which God can freely and peacefully dwell.

God's overall ideal of absolute True Love is realized and perfected through humankind in a vertical parent-child relationship. God created Adam first. He was to be the son of God and at the same time the substantial body of God Himself. Later, God created Eve as the object of Adam so that Adam and Eve could perfect the ideal of horizontal love, which is conjugal love. Eve was to be the daughter of God, and also, as a bride she was to substantially perfect the ideal of the horizontal love of God.

The place in which Adam and Eve are perfected, consummating their first love by marrying under the blessing of God, is precisely the place where God meets His substantial bride. This is because God's ideal of absolute love descends vertically and joins where the ideal of conjugal love between Adam and Eve is realized horizontally. The True Love of God and the True Love of humankind join and perfect themselves at the same point, although they came from different directions, one vertical and the other horizontal."

The same truth that we see in the Divine Principle also appears in the words of True Father. Adam is the body of God. Taking the body of Adam, God seeks his spouse. Eve is the daughter of God and his bride. The marriage of God happens through the body of Adam and Eve, which is why the marriage of Adam and Eve is the marriage between the two halves of God. At the same time it is the marriage between the two halves of the universe. Through the experience of "first love" (the original love that is experienced in the direct dominion of God), heaven and earth, positivity and negativity, spiritual world and physical world become one body or one entity.

When the man experiences "first love", God experiences it at the same time. This is the point where he meets his work of creation. Through the marriage of True Parents, for the first time, God saw the fulfilment of his work of creation after a long wait throughout history.

Human beings evolved the concept that God is much greater, higher and distant from mankind, but through the words of True Father, we know now that we are the body of God and He wants to dwell within our hearts.

The perfect couple has five values:

1. *the centre of the dominion*
2. *the centre of harmony*
3. *the centre of the goodness*
4. *the heart of the truth and*
5. *the centre of the original mind.*

As well as defining individual perfection, those values of the couple are perfected universal patterns that every human being should complete. This is not a religious explanation, is the principle that came to exist before any religion, from the beginning of the creation of God. If it were a religious belief, we could decide to believe it or not, and accept it or not. But it is a spiritual principle that applies to every human being, just as the law of gravity, a physical law applies to every human being on earth. If an object is denser than air, releasing it will allow it to fall. It does not make sense to deny this.

This explanation in the Divine Principle is also one of the major parts to understand for completing the "Formula Course". The purpose of which is to reach the level at which we have eliminated all fallen nature and sins. By growing the four great realms of heart, we can experience "First Love" by perfectly resonating with God and feeling deep heavenly joy.

Knowing that, even when we go through difficulties and make sacrifices in our lives of faith, we will not be discouraged once we have it clear in our minds that the purpose of these difficulties and sacrifices is to become a person who can experience the "first love" between the couple and God and receive the infinite source of heavenly joy. Sometimes after carrying out many activities (e.g. participating in the Sunday Service, giving tithes, joining mobilizations, etc.), we can become tired and feel the need to complain. In this moment, we must remember that the purpose of all the activities is to free us from fallen natures and sins, becoming people who can experience heavenly joy. Regardless of the activity in which we are involved, we can keep our moods high in the anticipation of reaching that goal.

Looking at the structure of the four position foundation, if Adam or Eve grew vertically in the direction of the heart of God, at the same time they would approach each other horizontally. As they become closer to God, the love they experience between each other reaches a higher level and they are happier. At the last moment in the perfection of a couple, God, the husband and the wife become one body. This is the point of union of a perfected couple, where they can feel their first love and where there is a resonance between the perfect couple and God. In this situation, when the husband expresses his love for his wife, she will feel the love of God and vice-versa. Within human love will be the love of God and the love of Man will become Divine Love.

Once we experience this, it will be the Kingdom of Heaven here on Earth. The Principle of Creation explains that it is not necessary to go to the spiritual world to experience the Kingdom of Heaven. It is possible to experience it with the physical body here on earth. But, if you have fallen nature and sin, there will not be perfect resonance between couples, although they may try continuously. For example, although someone taps two bells, if they are far enough apart, there will be no resonance between them.

We learn that at each level of God's creation, from particles, atoms, molecules, minerals, plants, animals up to mankind, there is positivity and negativity that are manifestations of God's attributes. Through this principle, we can understand that God has a passionate nature with all the couples who are looking for maximum happiness. That is why, in the creation, he sought the completion of marriage, using the body of Adam to meet his intended spouse, Eve.

Within the Home Group, we set a "Weekly Goal" and try to improve daily the couple's relationship, aiming to achieve the maximum joy of conjugal love. What makes the Home Group become an interesting activity is not the food, or the coffee break, or the discussion. If the Home Group had only those elements, joy would not last a long time. Home Groups are interesting because it is through daily growth, we renew the conviction that one day in the future we will become our ideal couple.

The Third Blessing

The Divine Principle explains that the third blessing is made when a person sets the four position foundation centred on the dominion of God, by means of the action of giving love and receiving beauty between Man (substantial object in the image of God) and the whole of creation (substantial object symbolic of God).

Through the perfect union of a couple together with God, all creation can also receive the love of God. Father Moon explained that if a flower was in front of a perfect couple, it would be happy because it would be receiving the love of God through this couple.

God has true love that is absolute, unique, eternal and unchanging. On the other hand, God has no hatred or resentment. To become an image of God, man must have true love that is absolute, unique, eternal and unchanging, equal to God. That is why, if man manifests fallen nature, he will be failing in the realization of the ideal of creation itself and cannot become the image of God. If you have fallen nature and sin, God cannot stay with such a person. The Bible records that God expelled Adam and Eve from the garden, but understanding about God's creation, we can say that it was Adam and Eve who chased Him out, because God could not dwell in their bodies because of their sins and fallen natures.

Love and Beauty (subject and object)

Imagine a case where the husband and wife begin to discuss, because each one wants to do a different activity. The husband insists on his own opinion using as an argument that the Divine Principle says that the man is the subject and why women have to obey him. Could it be that this husband has a correct understanding about the position and function of the subject, as explained in the Divine Principle?

According to the Divine Principle, when two bodies that are the substantial form of the division of the dual characteristics of God, lay down a four position foundation and form a reciprocal base for the purpose of giving and receiving action, there are forces in operation between the subject and the object to unite them as the third object of God. In this situation, the definition of love is an emotional force given by the subject to the object and the definition of beauty is an emotional force given by the object to the subject. The power of love is active and the stimulation of beauty is passive.

Some examples:
In the relationship between God and Man, God gives love as subject, in so far as Man returns beauty as an object. Between a man and a woman, the man is the subject that gives love just as the woman is the object that returns beauty. In the universe as a whole, Man is the subject that gives love and the rest of creation is the object that responds with beauty.

The Divine Principle continues to explain: "When the subject and the object are united, a love appears that is latent in both beauty and also beauty that is latent in love. This is because, when the subject and the object are brought together in circular motion, the subject may be in the position of object and the object in the position of subject".

When they are completely united in one body by love, the subject and object make a circular or spherical motion and in this dynamic movement, we cannot distinguish who is the subject or who is the object. The subject can freely assume the position of object and the object the position of subject. For example, in a discussion between two people the positions of subject and object are unrestricted and constantly changing; that's why they can continue the discussion. In this way, when you have unity through love, the relationship between the subject and the object may become something dynamic. Although the subject assumes the position of object, because of love, it will maintain its value. If love is present in the relationship of subject and object, no conflicts will arise from the differences between the positions.

For example, when children play "horsey-horsey", mounted on the backs of the parents, although parents are tired, they feel joy to serve their children from the position of object. It would be very strange if the parents wanted to climb on the backs of the children by saying that because they are in the position of subject and the children in the position of object the children are the ones who should serve the parents. Even when in the role of object, allowing the children ride on their backs, the parents feel joy and don't lose value because internally they are the "subject of love". On the other hand, the hearts of the children already feel the value and position that the parents have. Because of love, all are happy, independent of the positions that they are dealt with in that moment.

When we interpret the Divine Principle without applying love, it can be interpreted in a wrong way, such as in the example in which the husband insists that the wife must obey him because he is in the position of a subject.

Within the Home Group, our concept of leadership is that the leader must "serve" the other, just as True Father explains: "With the heart of parents in the shoes of a servant"

The Human Portion of Responsibility

In the Principle of Creation the words of the "three great blessings" appear; "*Be fruitful, multiply and have dominion*". Based on those words from God the human portion of responsibility began. Perfection or not, depends on acceptance and completion of the human portion of responsibility. Man grows and matures not only by the force of the principle, but also by their own human portion of responsibility during the period of growth.

God has 95% of the responsibility and Man has a 5% portion. God does not interfere with Man's responsibility in this aspect. By fulfilling the responsibility that even God cannot interfere with, and participating in the work of God's creation, Man will acquire the two positions of creator and that of having dominion. Ultimately, Man acquires the value of the Child of God.

In the beginning, God wanted Man to inherit the position of creator and have dominion. But just as God can only dominate the world because he is its creator, for Man to become lord of creation, he also needs to be a creator. So that Man can participate in the work of creation, God does not do the full 100 %. He deliberately left a part unfinished and thus gave Man the responsibility to create that part. Where was the part of the creation which God left unfinished so that the man could finish it? That part was within Man himself. Although Man was not able to create the world, nor even a small part of his own physical body, he would create himself, perfecting his love, thus achieving individual perfection. When Man reaches perfection, once a part of the world, he would be participating together with God in the work of creation and thus could obtain the position of creator and consequently the ruler (owner or lord of creation). Also, the human portion of responsibility was given by God in order for Man to inherit the value and position of creator and have dominion. The essence of the human portion of responsibility is the perfection of love.

The heart of God to give his share of responsibility to Man could be compared to the heart of a mother who is teaching her daughter to make a toy teddy bear. The mother designs and makes almost all of the bear and only leaves a part of the eye unfinished so that the child can participate in the design and complete the making of it. Then she holds the child's hand and helps her design and attach the eye that was missing. To give joy to her child that mother praises her saying that it was she who designed it and made it. This is the same situation as the heart of God.

God allowed Man to participate in his work of creation in order to relate as his children, differentiating them from the angels. In this way, we can understand that the human portion of responsibility is not a burden, but a blessing from God.

To achieve the goal of the three great blessings and avoid the fall, God gave his Word to man; this was the commandment "do not eat". By observing and obeying this commandment, man can fulfil the human portion of responsibility to achieve the three great blessings.

In the "Resurrection" Divine Principle explains that if God hadn't given the Word, there would be no "human portion of responsibility ". To give the Word is the responsibility of God; believing the Word and practicing it is the responsibility of Man (This is one of the 4 principles of resurrection). Although we want to fulfil human responsibility, if God does not give the Word it cannot exist. Also it is God who decides to whom to give responsibility. God gave it to Man and not to the angels. Although the archangel also committed sin, the concern of God was for Man, because only Man received their share of the responsibility. If God gave spiritual sensitivity to the archangel, it would mean that he would be giving a portion of responsibility to the archangel also.

In the beginning, God had 100% of the responsibility in his hands and he decided to give a portion of responsibility to Man in order to give him the value of creator, ruler (owner) and child of God. Once he divided and gave a portion to Man, only when the two parts met, would it be possible to carry out 100%. If Man failed, God would also be failing in the realization of 100% of the common goal.

The Nature of the Human Portion of Responsibility

First of all you must have the intent, purpose and will of God in relation to the human portion of responsibility. This means that it is not what Man decides to do that becomes the human portion of responsibility. To clarify his intention, God needs to give the word: "Be fruitful, multiply and have dominion" and "do not eat". Man needs to believe and practice that word as it was given.

Second, the word "portion" means that at first 100% of the responsibility was in the hands of God and He separated a small part (5 %) and gave it to Man to enable them to "participate" in his work of creation.

Therefore, we know that there is a "human portion of responsibility" but first there was "God's portion of responsibility". The word "portion" indicates that on God's part, in search of the realization of a common goal, the intention to share the responsibility with Man always existed. As a result, the only way for Man to participate in the work of God's creation is to achieve his own perfection.

Third, a growth period is necessary to complete the human portion of responsibility. If it were not for this time period after God created Adam, then we would already be perfect, without having the chance to show compliance with the human portion of responsibility. For that reason God gave the growth period, creating the world with time and space. The purpose of the human portion of responsibility is to enable man to reach individual perfection followed by the second and third blessings.

Fourth, the human portion of responsibility is to give Man the position of creator and ruler, as the son of God.

The human portion of responsibility is not a debt repayment. It is a small condition to substantiate the value of man. The motivation for God to give the human portion of responsibility was love. Therefore, we can understand that indemnity conditions are not punishments, rather they are conditions to retrieve the value that Man lost, because the origin of the concept of the condition of indemnity is the human portion of responsibility. God gave us indemnity conditions because he *loves us*, his children.

Definition of the Human Mind

The conscience of an original man is the result of the action of giving and receiving between the divine mind and physical mind centred on the **Truth**. The original mind is the result of the action of giving and receiving between the divine mind and physical mind centred on **God**. In the original world, the directions of the desires of the conscience are the same directions of the original mind and of God.

The evil mind is the result of the action of giving and receiving between the spiritual mind and the physical mind centred on Satan, therefore, such a person always displays the opposite direction to the will of God.

The conscience of a fallen man is centred on what he thinks is good. That's why the conscience of a fallen man can go in different directions, sometimes in agreement or sometimes against God's will. This is something that fallen man does not know. Until they come to perfection, fallen man must not rely solely on their conscience.

Between two people of conscience, conflicts can occur; because each one is centred on what he thinks is right. The conscience of fallen man is not absolute, but is relative. That is why despite the fact that there are two people of conscience they can be in conflict. For example, the same thing may seem right in the eyes of one person and wrong in the eyes of another. Conflict can happen between two church members with different views in spite of the fact that both want to act in line with the providence.

When True Father explains about the conscience, he is referring to the conscience of original man, or the original mind.

The Providence of Restoration

The "Providence of Restoration" means God's providence to restore fallen man to his original state endowed at the creation, thus fulfilling the purpose of creation.

Externally performing activities such as for example, setting up a factory, with the purpose to support any activity of True Parents, may also be called "Providence", as long as they are asking for a providential reason. But within the definition of the Providence of Restoration, is the concept that fallen man needs to return to his original state. For this reason, despite being involved with external activities, if that part is missing, is not called the providence of restoration in the full sense. In addition, if we are concerned about external achievements, we must also be concerned with the development of love, personal growth, unity of couples and my own realization of the three great blessings. This is the concept and definition of the Providence of Restoration. We must avoid separating the concepts of "external activities" and "my development of love". When we do any external activity, we must always remember the importance of the internal growth that must be achieved through such activity.

Pattern of Salvation (The Purpose of the Formula Course)

Sometimes people have a limited vision of what salvation will be. Each denomination has its own idea, or their own way. A person may think that feeling the Holy Spirit in the middle of worship is a kind of salvation and another may think that some other experience is the pattern of salvation. Whatever, it is only one part of the process of salvation. Then, what is the more complete explanation of salvation? We, as Unificationists, our response is "salvation is restoration". Then, let's imagine that we are explaining this to a new guest, and he asks us "what is restoration?" What would our response be? If we only give a response that goes round in circles by saying that "salvation is restoration" and "restoration is salvation", in the end, we do not have a clear explanation.

What is restoration? Restoration is to return to the original state. Then it is likely that the guest will ask "What is the original state?" The answer may be "the original state is the situation before the fall." Then, "what was the situation before the fall?" "It is the original situation". "What is the original situation?" "Original ...?" and so on. If we do not understand Principle in a more practical way, we cannot use our understanding to bear witness and to practice Principle in real life.

In conclusion, if we do not clarify the "purpose", we will not come to the answer. The process of salvation is completed when we fulfil the purpose of the creation. Specifically, the original state is reached when, the pattern of individual development, followed by completion of the Second and the Third Blessing, as was shown above. This is the clear and specific goal for all of us. This is the pattern for entering the Kingdom of Heaven. This is the explanation that all religions in history wanted to hear. Today we have this content in our hands.

According to the Divine Principle, to save a patient is to restore their health to the state they were in before getting ill. To save a drowning man is to restore him to his original position before he began to choke. To save a fallen man, with sin, means to restore him to the original position without sin which he enjoyed in the beginning.

To understand what should be done, man needs to understand what the final goal is. The ultimate goal is the realization of the three great blessings: Uniting mind and body, becoming a person that feels the joy of God, becoming the temple of God, reaching divinity and forming a single body with him. Then, through unity in perfected marriage, we can feel the joy and love of God within the family by multiplying children and extending their joy to the level of society, nation and world. In this way we may engage in the act of giving and receiving of love and beauty with all creation and establish a world full of joy.

Completing this is the kingdom of heaven on earth. This is the fuller explanation concerning salvation. This is the goal of the life of faith that all must achieve and the goal of the formula course of restoration. The purpose of Home Groups is to achieve this goal.

Direct Dominion (the concept of "master" and the pattern of the Kingdom of Heaven)

The Direct Dominion of God is the Kingdom of Heaven and our destination through Home Groups.

As defined in the Divine Principle, the Direct Dominion is:

1. *centred on God where*
2. *subject and object become a united body,*
3. *lay down the four position foundation*
4. *in perfect unity with the heart of God and*
5. *in accordance with the will of the subject*
6. *make perfect action of giving and receiving of love and beauty between them*
7. *for the purpose of goodness.*

"Direct Dominion" is the name of the state where all this has been fulfilled.

In the secular world, people are accustomed to using the word "dominion" or "dominate" in another sense. Usually, when you hear the word "dominate", in the case of fallen man, you can imagine something like dictatorship, exploitation, or something in that direction. But the Divine Principle introduces the concept of "dominion" with a different meaning. Dominion is a situation that exemplifies the action of giving and receiving of love and beauty, becoming a single body, centred on the will of the subject that has made perfect unity of heart with God, thus completing the purpose of goodness. The realization of such a perfect action of giving and receiving is the way to master. "Dominion" occurs in a situation in which one feels free to love and someone else feels free to return beauty, freely alternating the positions and developing joy with the other. When the action of giving and receiving love becomes perfect, dominion is also perfect. In this way, if you increase dominion, joy increases further and freedom never decreases. This is dominion by love. In this case the more one receives dominion; the more one is happy and free. This concept of dominion is different from that well-known in the secular world.

When Adam and Eve exchange love and beauty, God remains in the midst of them and experiences love along with them. If Man has fallen nature, the resonance of love between God, man and woman does not occur, and of course neither does the "Direct Dominion of God".

Direct Dominion of God for Man and the Direct Dominion of Man for all things

Examples of the Direct Dominion of God for man:

1. *centred on God,*
2. *Adam and Eve become one united body,*
3. *Set out the base of four family positions,*
4. *in perfect unity with the heart of God,*
5. *in accordance with the will of God centred on Adam,*
6. *make perfect action of mutually giving and receiving of love and beauty between them,*
7. *are living the life of goodness.*

This is called the "Direct Dominion" of God over Man. In this relationship between God, Adam and Eve, it is not clear who is dominating who, God dominating Adam and Eve or Adam and Eve dominating God. In reality, both are happening at the same time.

When the Divine Principle explains that the Direct Dominion is in accordance with the will of Adam (subject), husbands may think that their wives must always obey their instructions. But the Divine Principle does not say that it accepts the will of any type of Adam (subject). Immediately after this part, the Divine Principle continues the explanation by saying that the "Adam should be centred on God". This Adam (subject) must be perfect and must be perfectly united in heart with God.

The part where it says "2) Adam and Eve are a perfect united body," refers to the first and second blessing. Through personal development and unity of a perfect couple, we can experience the Direct Dominion of God. This happens only with the completion of the human portion of responsibility. In this area of the Direct Dominion of God, He is in man and man is in Him.

These 7 points clearly show what the Kingdom of Heaven is, there are no symbols or parables, and it is also a full explanation of salvation. Once human beings live like that there would be no end to our happiness.

It is important to understand that this plan of the Direct Dominion of God is the goal of our life, just as is the "Formula Course". All our activities are opportunities for us to reach this goal.

The Divine Principle continues to explain that such a man that lives in the direct dominion of God 1) understands and experiences the heart of God, 2) fully understands God's will and 3) practices the will of God. In this condition, the relationship between God and man is similar to the relationship between the mind and body.

For example, at the moment when the mind of a man wants to grasp an object, his body grasps it immediately, when God wishes something, the man likewise realizes immediately.

The Direct Dominion of man over all things occurs when,

1. *centred on God,*
2. *perfected man and the world of all things (as object) are one unified body,*
3. *establishing the four position foundation,*
4. *in accordance with the will of the man who is joined completely with God in heart,*
5. *makes perfect action of giving and receiving of love and beauty between the man and the world of all things and*
6. *fulfilling the purpose of goodness.*

When they complete all of these conditions, this is called the direct dominion of man over all things. This equates to the third Blessing. After we have completed all these conditions, by entering the direct dominion, the joy of the three great blessings will remain in the spiritual world and we will be able to live in eternal heavenly joy.

Indemnity Conditions

In the "General Introduction," the Divine Principle explains that man is in a state of conflict between the original mind and the evil mind within himself, and this is the source of conflict within couples, the families, societies, nations and the world.

Before the fall, in the original state, man had a single subject, God. But after the fall, man was placed in a midway position between God and Satan. This is a position outside of the Principle. God is the Father and creator, but Satan is also a father because he has the condition as an initiator of a blood lineage.

Man is in the midway position between God and Satan. Restoration occurs through indemnity conditions. If a person performs good actions, he establishes indemnity conditions and makes it possible to separate from Satan and get closer to God's Dominion. On the other hand, when he commits sin, he comes into a state of accusation by Satan and distances himself from God, increasing the dominion of Satan. That which increases the dominion of God is a condition of indemnity and that which increases the dominion of Satan is a condition of accusation. Indemnity conditions exist for the separation of Satan. And these indemnity conditions are a form of the human portion of responsibility.

So what does "restoration through indemnity" really mean? When something loses its position or original state, certain conditions must be established for the position or the original state to be restored. The establishment of such conditions is called "indemnity". For example: to restore loss of honour, position, health or friendship, we must establish the conditions necessary by making sincere effort, achieving good grades and receiving adequate medical care. Let's suppose that there are two people who once loved each other, but now they are in a bad situation. For them to restore the original state of love with each other, they must establish the condition of mutual apology. Similarly, the man, who lost his position or original state endowed at the creation, should establish necessary conditions in order to restore himself. This act of returning to the position of the original state endowed at the creation by making a condition is called "restoration by indemnity". The condition to be established for restoration through indemnity is called an "indemnity condition ". The providence of restoration by establishing conditions is called "the providence of restoration by indemnity".

When we give lectures to new guests, sometimes they don't understand this part of the content. For example, when the lecturer explains about how to establish indemnity conditions, and writes down: the central figure is such and such a person, the conditional object is 40 minutes prayer, the time period is 40 days and the purpose is to restore a spiritual child, people can be confused thinking we are offering of some kind of spiritual ritual, saying that it is the same thing that they do by establishing central figure - themselves, the conditional object is any animal offering, period remains some time and the purpose is to get a bride. In this case, what is the difference between the "condition of indemnity" and the "spiritual ritualistic offering" with a personal purpose? Certainly we understand that they are different concepts. But, how do we clearly explain the essential difference?

Let's think of another example. A guest at the workshop heard that a car accident could be indemnity for something in the past. When you hear this part of the seminar, you might think you understand evil and say that this is the same thing that your church teaches and that this is called a "curse". He might conclude also: there are curses and blessings in a life of faith. Then, "indemnity" must be the same thing as that "curse". If a person does something good, God blesses you and if you do something bad, God punishes you. When we hear this, we know that this understanding is wrong. But, do we clearly understand what the essential difference is?

The source of indemnity is part of human responsibility. In the original world, the man needs to fulfil his part of the responsibility to reach perfection. This is the process going from zero to a positive. After the fall, mankind lost the original position and needs to fulfil his human portion of responsibility to return to the original state. For this to happen, man needs to establish a providence of indemnity. This is the process of going from less than the zero point (= the point before you began the sin). Then, the essence of an indemnity condition is the human portion of responsibility. An "indemnity condition" is the name of the "human portion of responsibility" in the process of going from less than zero to retrieve the lost value.

Then the indemnity condition has the same nature as the human portion of responsibility. Remembering again the natures of the special parts of human responsibility are: 1) first, there is a specific intention and purpose for God to give a share of the responsibility for man, 2) has the notion of allowing people to participate in his work of creation, 3) has the goal of individual perfection, 4) has God's intention to give the position of creator and sovereign to man as his son. On the other hand, the concept of "spiritual ritual" and the idea of "curse" are not based on these 4 points. This is a big difference.

As we can see, if we do not understand the exact meaning of the "human portion of responsibility", we will not understand the exact meaning of "indemnity". The condition of indemnity is different from the concept of punishment, curse, fines, suffering, etc., but, it is a condition that God gave Man with the motivation and intention of love enabling them to retrieve their value.

Everyone in society uses the word "responsibility" or "be responsible" daily. But, when ordinary people use these words, they fail to understand in the same sense as with the 4 points about the nature of the human portion of responsibility that were previously explained. There is a difference between the "human portion of responsibility" that we use in the Divine Principle and "responsibility" commonly used in society.

Just as human responsibility is not a penalty, neither is a condition of indemnity, it is not punishment, it is not something bad. Human responsibility is the blessing of God to enhance human beings as creator, sovereign and child of God. Then indemnity conditions are to restore the value that was lost due to the fall. God, in loving his children, wants to give them some condition to restore the value that was lost when man made a mistake.

We are going to give you an example. Imagine that there is a car accident and the central figure says that it is indemnity. In fact, sometimes an accident could really occur because of indemnity, but in many cases we do not know whether it was indemnity or not, or if it was just a driver error. Hearing this, a new member may decide wrongly about indemnity, thinking that indemnity is defined as something bad. Also when a central figure gives a day of fasting as a condition of indemnity for a member who had made a mistake, the member may make the wrong conclusion about indemnity, thinking that the meaning of indemnity is punishment. This kind of misunderstanding about the true meaning of certain points of the Divine Principle causes many difficulties and conflicts and even sometimes allows resentment to emerge between us in our day to day life of faith. To avoid these problems, we must understand correctly the definition of each concept in Divine Principle.

The Divine Principle explains that there are three grades of payment of indemnity conditions: the same value, of a lower value and of a higher value.

How must people fulfil indemnity conditions? It has to be through a reverse course. In the Divine Principle we read that the chosen nation of Israel rejected and crucified Jesus. Therefore, in order to make a reverse course, we should love Jesus, carry the cross and follow him. This is the way to restore failures of the past through indemnity by following a reverse course, returning to the original position. Mankind caused God to grieve by rebelling against him and falling in corruption. Therefore, to be restored through indemnity, people must reverse their fallen nature and comfort God, and be restored to the condition of mankind with original nature endowed at creation, practising the will of God. The first Adam rebelled against God, thus forcing his descendants to fall into the embrace of Satan. Jesus, who came as the second Adam, therefore had to serve and honour God from the position of being abandoned by Him, in order to be able to restore all humanity from the realm of Satan to God. Likewise, we should do the opposite of the failures of the past.

Who should make indemnity conditions? Mankind themselves must do so. The only the reason for an indemnity condition is because of the human portion of responsibility, so Man is responsible for doing this, not God, not Satan, nor the creation. God gave the 5% portion to Man. The first human ancestors fell under the dominion of Satan. Therefore, in order that Man may be restored to the position of Satan's master, Man himself must establish the proper condition of indemnity through the fulfilment of his own portion of responsibility. Until Satan is under the dominion of Man, the human portion of responsibility does not end. Our Father subjugated and dominated Satan naturally and returned him to the original position. With true love, our Father completed his human portion of responsibility by following the reverse course in the place of Adam. This is the way to liberate God. It is not God who must do this. Mankind must do so, since God gave responsibility to Man. But, in practice, no fallen man could restore Satan and return him to God. True Father was the only one who carried out the hope of God. Neither can Satan return to God alone. The fate of God, of Satan, and of human beings, was entrusted to True Father. This is the impressive achievement of True Parents and is our pride. The Lord of the Second Coming is so precious to God and to humanity.

The Formula Course - 1 (from the Viewpoint of Formation, Growth and Completion)

The formula course is unique, but there are several perspectives to consider. We can deal with it in various ways, but the purpose is the same. The purpose of the formula course is the perfection of love.

In relation to the period of growth (formation, growth and completion), Adam and Eve should have grown to the level of individual perfection and entered into the direct dominion of God. But they fell and acquired original sin, losing their value and position, becoming fallen. From the position of fallen man, they need to retrieve the value and state that they had *immediately after* the fall. Besides going through the original formula course for the growth of heart, fallen man needs to remove fallen nature and sin with a course for the separation of Satan, a course of indemnity. At the same time that you need to bring out your original heart, you need to decrease sin and fallen nature until you return to the situation that Adam and Eve were in immediately after the fall (only with the original sin, without fallen nature, without collective or hereditary or individual sin and with the original heart grown until around 14 to 16 years of age). After that, you should receive the Messiah, remove the original sin and experience for 7 years the original formula course for perfection, together with the Messiah, experiencing the heart of that original period that Adam and Eve did not experience due to the fall. This completes the formula course by entering the direct dominion of God.

The Formula Course - 2 (from the Viewpoint of the Eight Vertical Levels)

This is an explanation of the same formula course from another viewpoint; from the point of view of the 8 levels. The 8 levels (vertical) are a servant of servant, servant, adopted child, illegitimate child (or step-child), child, mother, father and God. Originally man was born as the son of God, but, because of the fall, man has distanced himself in heart from the heart of God. The 8 levels are also not external hierarchies in the church. For example, it would be a mistake for a person to think that someone in the position of leader has already surpassed the position of servant of servants due to the position he occupies externally. The title "servant of servants" means that he is very far from the heart of God. After improving himself spiritually, developing his love, eliminating his fallen nature and drawing close to the heart of God he can go to the position of "servant". The feeling of a person towards God from the level of "servant" is different from the feeling of the same person at the level of "adopted son".

After the fall mankind was placed in the position of "servant of a servant" in front of God. A typical test that occurs in one's life of faith in this position is to feel that your very existence is denied, since you do not have a direct relationship with God. You live, mistreated by Satan who is a "servant".

In the Old Testament times, Moses was still was in the position of "servant", as he had no merit of the age. He was approximately at the servant level of God's heart and had not yet felt the heart of God as a father. At the level of "servant", the focus of a person's training is obedience. He has to obey God completely and feels as if he were being forced to do things. This happens because he has not yet deeply restored his heart with God. By reason and logic he knows that God is a father of love, but his heart does not feel that. At this level you can feel that there is no freedom in your life of faith. In our experience, we frequently notice that a proportion of new people, at the beginning of their life of faith, feel that they have no freedom in the church, claiming that their central figure does not allow drinking beer, smoking etc., but when he grows spiritually, the situation changes and he cannot distinguish between the freedom of the evil mind and the freedom of the original mind. So we understand that a whether person feels they have freedom or not in a particular situation, depends a lot on the spiritual level of each one. The reason not to feel freedom can be within the person themselves and not in their circumstances.

When a person grows up to the position of "adopted son', he becomes more pure, approaching the heart of God, then he feels more freedom. An "adopted son" feels more appreciation and joy in his life of faith, even though he sacrifices much. At this level you know the love and the heart of God, calling out to God or Father, determining to live only in accordance with the will of God, feeling joy and courage to live with God and having a sense of gratitude. This is the situation of a person who came up to the position of 'adopted son" or the New Testament where the Old Testament equates to the position of "servant".

People can feel different levels of heart doing the same activity because the spiritual position of each may be different. Some feel like a "servant of servants", others like a "servant", and some as a "foster child", even though externally they are doing the same activities.

After removing the original sin through the Blessing, people feel they are "true children" of the direct lineage of God and that they have inherited God's heart and lineage. After experiencing the heart of a "son or daughter" they can experience the heart of "mother", "father" and "God". Getting up to the level of heart of "God" means that there is no distance of heart between the person and God. They are completely joined with the heart of God and what God feels is the same as the person feels. In other words, this is individual perfection.

It would be great if everyone could remember those 9 points of the pattern of individual perfection so as not to lose the focus of their life of faith from day to day.

Hell, or the Pre-Old Testament era represents the "servant of servant" level; the Old Testament, "servant"; the New Testament, "adopted child". After removing original sin, a person enters into the realm of "son" and continues to grow, restoring the 4 great kingdoms of heart. It is when you complete the entire experience of heart and love, becoming equal to God, as if you were the body of God that there are no missing elements to represent the heart of God through their life. If a glove has 4 fingers, it does not fit well on the hand and a person will feel uncomfortable. Similarly, if we do not have all the elements of the heart and love of God in us, God cannot feel good using our body and living with us. We must be the image and likeness of God and we should not have any natures that God does not have, for example: rage, hatred and resentment, etc.

Historically speaking, the time of Adam, Noah, Abraham and Moses, was the course of "servant of servants" and "servant". After the fall, man started from the position of "servant of servant" and recovered the distance from the heart of God, thanks to the victories of each central figure that paved that historical way. Jesus opened the way for all human beings to become "adopted children" and the Lord of the Second Advent has opened more than a way for man to become "true children" of the blood lineage of God.

The Formula Course - 3 (from the Viewpoint of the Three Great Blessings)

The goal of the formula course is the realization of the Three Great Blessings. If one completes all of the conditions of the Three Great Blessings then one can go to the spiritual world and continue to experience the level of happiness that comes from fulfilling the Three Great Blessings and so enter the Kingdom of Heaven.

Adam and Eve should have originally fulfilled their human portion of responsibility during the period of growth, passing through the periods of formation, growth and completion, as the formula course. What would have been the result if Adam and Eve had completed their human portion of responsibility? They would have reached the position of a creator and could dominate with love. Because of that position and value, they could begin to dominate all things (Third Blessing). Completion of the Third Blessing is perfection based on the realization of the First Blessing that is, individual perfection. And individual perfection is the outcome of fulfilling one's human portion of responsibility.

In the "Consummation of Human History" there is an explanation about the two types of dominion of all things: the internal dominion through the heart and external dominion through the use of science.

Through the realization of the First Love, Adam and Eve would have become one body with God, as well as True Parents who completed the final condition to become the True Parents of Heaven and Earth and Humankind. The point of union, the perfect couple, is the centre of dominion through love. All things want to receive God's love through the perfect couple who fulfilled the Second Blessing. So completion of the Third Blessing is based on realization of the Second Blessing.

The Divine Principle explains that when Man fulfils the First and Second Blessing, he enters into the direct dominion of God. Based on the fulfilment of the First and Second Blessings, creating all of the conditions required for fulfilling the Third Blessing, Man can master all things through the True Love of God. This is called the direct dominion of man over all things. This is the Kingdom of Heaven.

By fulfilling our human portion of responsibility, we graduate from the formula course to perform the Three Great Blessings by developing and refining our love.

The formula course is also the goal of the Home Groups. A Home Group does not become interesting because of the tea, or coffee, or the cake and talks, but rather because we can grow each day by following the formula course.

The concept of the formula course is not something vague, like "living for others is a good thing, do voluntary service, loving our neighbour is good too". On the contrary, it has a clear goal. The formula course is where Man qualifies to fulfil the Three Great Blessings.

The formula course in the fallen world is a little more complex than in the original world. Fallen man must go through two formula courses together, the original formula course for growth of the heart and the formula course to remove fallen nature and sin (the course of separation from Satan, that is to say, the course of indemnity)

The marriage blessing would have originally been granted after reaching individual perfection but fallen man receives the blessing at the perfection level of the growth stage to eliminate original sin, which is why he creates a family before completing individual perfection. In this case, Man needs to do two things at the same time: achieve unity as a couple, as a Blessed Family and achieve unity of mind and body for individual perfection. Thus, in our life of faith, we are passing through the course of individual perfection and blessed marriage at the same time.

Unity of mind and body will not happen only by disciplining the physical body by, for example, fasting, denying the desires of the flesh. It only occurs when we receive the huge energy of the love of God. Once Man receives the love of God, he feels a stronger stimulation than that of the desires of the flesh which is why he can overpower the desires of the physical body. This means that, before we can dominate the body, we must accept the dominion of God. But as fallen people we have fallen nature and sins that prevent the love of

God coming to us which is why it becomes difficult for the mind to dominate the body. We strive to remove fallen nature but, at the same time, we are looking for the unity of mind and body.

What is the relationship between the unity of Cain and Abel and the unity of mind and body? In the process of the relationship between Cain and Abel, we strive to love those who we feel are difficult to love and opportunities appear to remove the fallen nature. This becomes the process of developing love and facilitates the unity of mind and body. Many times we went through a type of test in our life of faith, as for example when we had to obey the direction of the central figure when we are very tired and did not want to sacrifice our physical body. At such a time we must overcome the negative thoughts that arise because of the willingness of the evil mind which is under the dominion of the desires of the body. When we overcome this by obeying the central figure, a love for God and his will is initiated in us. We are growing and overcoming our fallen nature through the power of vertical love. For example: a member has been sleeping after working hard all day and suddenly the central figure asks him to perform some activity; negative thinking arises in that moment and he does not feel any desire to obey. But, in striving to love God who works through this central figure, the person rises above and beyond difficulties presented by the physical body. While working on the union of Cain and Abel we are also going through the course of uniting our mind and body.

On the other hand, Abel also passes through the process of uniting his mind and body based on true love by sacrificing himself to love Cain. Increasing the union of mind and body will increase the flow of God's love which will facilitate victory in the achieving unity between Cain and Abel.

Uniting mind and body and eliminating fallen nature also facilitates building the connection between couples. Imagine if one of the spouses in a couple was already perfect; would that not facilitate creating a deep couple connection? On the other hand, striving for union of the couple also facilitates the union of mind and body. For example, when one of the spouses is put in a challenging situation, he has the opportunity to try to unite his mind and body by overcoming anger, controlling his fallen nature and loving the enemy. This is an optimal opportunity to remove fallen nature. This is the secret: the union of a couple helps the union of mind and the body and the union of mind and body helps the union of a couple.

Within the couple relationship one will see all of the contents that have not been overcome in the individual course. For example, if a person flees several times from the tests that appear in the relationship of Cain and Abel and the situations are not resolved before the blessing then the same tests will immediately reappear within the relationship with their spouse. In our course of life, God can change our central figure many times and if, by chance, we fail any test with any central figure, we will be able to overcome the same test with the other. But in the case of a spouse, this is a unique and eternal relationship and, even in the spiritual world, we will have to continue the process of restoring what was lacking in the formula restoration course.

There are two different situations in the process of moving through the formula course.

The first situation is to resolve, within a Cain and Abel relationship, the issue of loving, overcoming conflicts and removing fallen natures. Through dealing with several central figures, with different natures, the process of joining together and having love flowing between Cain and Abel is accelerated, fallen nature is removed and seeking of individual perfection is supported. If one can surmount these tests then one will have fewer tests when with their spouse and will have more strength to transcend the challenges that arise.

The second situation is the case of failing several times to create unity between Cain and Abel, trying to flee when the tests arise and ignoring the need for the unity of Cain and Abel. After marriage all the tests failed as a single person will reappear within the relationship of husband and wife.

The difficulty in overcoming the conflicts will be the same in the two cases. In the first case, the size of the challenge is divided between several different people (Abel or Cain) so, when you are in the conjugal relationship, most of the problems will already be overcome.

When we have several people to love on a day-to-day basis, whether Abel, Cain or guests, the greater the number of people we see the more we will have opportunities to open the love in us. For example, if we have 10 guests, then we can experience the education of God that allows us to eliminate the fallen nature and grow our love, overcoming conflicts with each of them. On the other hand, if we did not have a guest and do not try to love Cain or respond to the approach of Abel, we will not have many opportunities to develop love. But as God needs to save us, He will of course do his work in another way. In this situation, the size of the test that we need is the same; one will face a large test with a single person, our spouse and will therefore be much more difficult to overcome. It is always better to love Abel and Cain in the church and to love your guests by testifying. Then we can overcome difficulties within the couple through this process of the growth of love. If our love grows through these activities then we can give our best quality love to our spouse. On the other hand it is also the case that, if our love increases through the victory of conjugal love, then we can pass on this love to the members (Cain and Abel) or guests, thus facilitating our victory.

For an individual the union of mind and body, union of the couple, the relationship of Cain and Abel and perfection are not disconnected but are, on the contrary, intimately linked and the success of one directly influences success of the other. If you do not clearly understand the meaning of each part of the Divine Principle then is not possible to reach that level of understanding.

The way to complete the goal of the formula course of restoration is to fulfil the human portion of responsibility and the essence of the human portion of responsibility is growth of and perfection of love.

The Formula Course - 4 (from the Viewpoint of the Foundation of Faith, the Foundation of Substance and the Foundation to Receive the Messiah)

The Divine Principle teaches that by going through the reverse course we must restore conditions in the form of the Three Great Blessings, in the order of the Third, Second and First Blessing.

How do we establish the Foundation of Faith? We can do it through making a "symbolic offering". Stating that historically: the "symbolic offering" to establish the basis of faith was needed before Moses. The elements for establishing the Foundation of Faith are: the "Central Figure", the "Conditional Object" and the "Time Period". The element "Symbolic Offering", i.e. the "Material Offering" appears here. That is why most religions emphasize the need for material contributions for people to be restored to the original state.

Through making a symbolic offering we can establish the "Condition of indemnity to restore all things" and "Condition of indemnity to restore man symbolically". When we are establishing the "Condition of indemnity to restore all things", this is a condition of Third Blessing type, but this does not mean literally fulfilling the Third Blessing.

The symbolic offerings are material offerings. When we make material offerings we are establishing two conditions at the same time: 1) Restoring all things to God and, at the same time, 2) Restoring ourselves because making of material offerings means that the man is returning to God through the material that is closest to God, because the material did not fall.

The purpose of establishing the Foundation of Faith is to establish the Foundation of Substance. We can establish the Foundation of Substance doing the "Condition of indemnity to eliminate fallen nature". Man should have reached divinity, but acquired fallen nature, that is why we need to some condition to remove it. Wc can do this through making a substan tial offering. A substantial offering means that Abel offers Cain to God. In other words Cain returns to God through Abel. Concerning the substantial offering, we are making the "Condition of indemnity to restore the children" and the "Condition of indemnity to restore the parents" at the same time. These are the conditions associated with the Second and First Blessing, but this does not mean that we literally fulfil the Second and the First Blessing.

What is the way to establish the Foundation of Substance? It is by making the substantial offering. In other words, we can establish it by making the "Condition of indemnity to eliminate fallen nature ". What is the practical way to establish this condition? We can make it by practising something that represents the reverse course by which fallen nature emerged. For example, when a person feels difficulty in taking the point of view of God by loving Abel he should strive to maintain his position of trying to return to God through Abel. When one wants to demonstrate the fallen nature of criticizing Abel, seeking in this way to dominate, one must strive to do the opposite, allowing oneself be dominated by Abel. And also, when one has the desire to multiply evil by speaking ill of Abel, against Abel's will in a fallen way, one should strive to grow in love, to multiply goodness. These are practical examples that occur on a day-to-day basis where we can go the reverse course and set the "Condition of indemnity to remove the fallen nature".

Each one of us is simultaneously in the positions of Cain and Abel, that is to say, in front of one person we are Cain and in front of someone else we are Abel. There is nobody that has only one fixed position. Then all people can practice this reverse course in their daily life.

Establishment of the Foundation of Substance can occur through the simple things that we practice on a day to day basis. For example, when a person feels wounded in heart from what a central figure said and the desire arises to speak ill of them, going the reverse course is speak positively about the Central Figure. To do this may only take about 10 seconds but it will be establishing a condition to establish the Foundation of Substance.

These small victories of making the conditions to create a Foundation of Substance that we accumulate on a day to day basis are converted into a condition to restore our spiritual children through witnessing.

Fallen man usually just speaks out what is in his mind at the time he thinks it, allowing fallen nature to reign, but he must master himself, fighting against the will of the ungodly mind. The greater part of practising fallen natures is done through the mouth. When we are provoked by someone, we must not release the words that come to mind in a moment of anger. If we can resist this then we will be avoiding multiplication of evil, and if we multiply good then that will be even better. This type of condition is not just a condition of faith if it is a condition that substantially eliminates our fallen nature. The process and how to establish the "Condition of indemnity to eliminate fallen nature" is to practice the opposite to what our fallen nature dictates.

In the Home Group we have opportunities to practice this by establishing a "Weekly Goal"; for example, a couple who fight a lot are determined to reduce their arguments and make a "Weekly Goal" to do this. They have been fighting often in the beginning, but if they succeed in complying with the "Weekly Goal ", the fighting will gradually decline. Eight fights per week will become only seven, then six and then five, four, three, two, one, and finally a point will be reached where there is an end to fighting altogether. And this period without fights then lasts for one month, two months etc. ... They say that their relationship has improved a lot compared to previously, developing now from feeling they are in Hell into a situation in which they do not fight any more, and are very happy. They do not believe that this could be possible before having this experience, but now they see that it is possible after they made it happen through the Home Group.

If this couple did not know how to practically use the Divine Principle they could have broken the Blessing long before. We can receive great benefits through the words of True Parents.

The purpose of the Home Group is to do this. When a member reaches at least a small victory through the "Weekly Goal", the Home Group and the life of faith of this member becomes more interesting and happy.

We will need our "Weekly Goal" for as long as we have not yet reached perfection. It is our goal on Earth, before we die, to become a perfected individual and also to achieve the union of a couple, which is the most important issue as a condition to live in the Kingdom of Heaven.

By making the Foundation of Faith and the Foundation of Substance, we can make the Foundation to receive the Messiah. The purpose of receiving the Messiah is to remove Original Sin. The Foundation of Substance is the condition of indemnity to restore ourselves to the position of children and parents. After the Fall, Adam became the representative of both good and evil, which is why God cannot deal with Adam directly. Abel was to lay the Foundation of Faith in the place of Adam and was placed in the position of the Central Figure for achieving the Foundation of Substance. After that, Abel should have the heart of Cain through love and sacrifice.

On the other hand, Cain must return to the side of God, overcoming the apparent lack of love. Cain must make the "Condition of indemnity to remove the fallen nature" by going the reverse course, opposite to what his fallen nature dictates, taking the point of view of God according to Abel, not reversing dominion but instead multiplying good. If Cain overcomes the feeling of lack of love, thus eliminating his fallen nature, the family of Adam will be completing the "Condition of indemnity to restore the children". And since Cain represents one half of Adam's nature, when the union of Cain and Abel occurs then God will also be restoring Adam (restoration of the parents) at the same time. Through making the substantial offering, obtaining the victory of love between Cain and Abel, the condition to restore the position of children and parents is made. This is the core content of the Foundation of Substance.

Abel represents Adam and Cain represents Lucifer, then the two together should restore the failure of the past. They must practice the opposite of what happened in the past according the Law of the Restoration by Indemnity. If a person does not understand his situation providentially his point of view of the relationship between Cain and Abel may become very superficial. For example, Abel is the person who gives the orders and Cain is the person who must obey everything. This is a mistaken view of the reality of the relationship between Cain and Abel.

In many respects, we can summarize the above by saying that the mission of Cain is to overcome the lack of love and the mission of Abel is to help Cain overcome it. Abel must restore the right of primogeniture (the right, by law or custom, of the legitimate, first-born son to inherit his parent's entire or main estate) through natural subjugation of Cain, overcoming the lack of love and achieving victory. To do this Abel must do nothing other than to practice love and sacrifice.

Originally there was already the Foundation of Faith and the Foundation of Substance before the Fall. In order to make the Foundation of Faith, Adam should have observed the commandment of God and passed through the period of growth. On the basis of further substantial growth Adam should have achieved union with God, felt the heart of God, become the temple of God and have acquired the original nature of creation.

Fulfilling all of these conditions, Adam would have become a perfect man in the moment that he fulfilled his "Human portion of responsibility" through completion of the Foundation of Faith and the Foundation of Substance.

In the original world the Foundation of Faith is established by passing perfectly through the period of growth, experiencing the original heart and maintaining sexual purity according to the principle of "absolute sex" (receiving an absolute sex partner, practising absolute sexual life, practising absolute sexual love which we inherit from True Parents). And on the basis of the victorious Foundation of Faith we become the perfect incarnation of the word, that is, the substantial Word of God. In the original world completion of the Foundation of Faith would mean fulfilment of the Foundation of Substance at the same time.

Originally, Adam should have reached divinity, but because of the Fall he acquired fallen nature, failing as well to lay the Foundation of Substance. Adam became the dwelling place of Satan and did not observe the commandment for the required period of time. This is why, to restore the Foundation of Faith, what we need today is a Central Figure, the Conditional Object and a Time Period. We also need the Foundation of Substance as a condition to remove fallen nature. In the course of restoration we need to establish the Foundation to receive the Messiah.

Adam should have established two conditions to carry out the purpose of creation. He should have first laid the Foundation of Faith, that is, he should have obeyed the commandment of God not to eat the fruit of the tree of knowledge of good and evil. Later on, Adam should have passed through the growth period during which he should have fulfilled his own share of responsibility by setting this condition of faith.

The second condition that Adam should have set to accomplish the purpose of creation was to establish the Foundation of Substance (become the incarnation). If Adam had established the Foundation of Faith, passing through the growth period in faith and obedience to the commandment of God, he could have been combined into one body with God on that basis.

In other words, he could have established the Foundation of Substance (incarnation), thus becoming the "Perfect incarnation of the word", having embodied the original nature of creation.

Adam could have reached the state of being a perfect man with individuality, which was the first blessing of God to man.

The Formula Course - 5 (from the Viewpoint of Indemnity)

The course of indemnity and the original course are not two totally different things. The course of indemnity is never an obstacle but only supports the course for the growth of the heart and the original ideal.

When person commits sin the need arises to recover his/her original value through the payment of indemnity. In the process of conducting the "Formula Course", the "The original course for growth of the heart “and the "Course of indemnity" are made at the same time, with the same purpose. In any activity that we do, as soon as we start passing through an indemnity period, the conditions we make will be used to eliminate sin or any pay indemnity that exists and for this reason good results do not appear from our activities. But as soon as we have finished paying indemnity the results will begin appear. Finishing indemnity means that the debt has been paid and when we then continue to establish good conditions, the results will emerge.

Overview of the course we have to go

The Formula Course for All Human Beings

In the formula course for the individual, all must love Cain and Abel. Loving the central figure, eliminating fallen nature, overcoming the feeling of the lack of love, you can be victorious in the position of Cain. Our Father explained about the "character of the man who is victorious as Cain" (the one who can love a central figure of any characteristics). All have two positions. In front of one person we in the position of Cain while in front of another we are in the position of Abel. When in the position of Abel we should always love and win the heart of Cain naturally, restoring the right of primogeniture. For example, we must win the heart of our spiritual children. Concerning the position of Abel, our Father explained about, "the character of the person who is *victorious* as Abel" (the one who can love Cain of any quality).

We must love and restore 3 to 12 spiritual children representing the 3 archangels of Adam and Eve and make them into 3 disciples. Before receive the Blessing we all need 3 spiritual children. If we do not receive the blessing on the basis of a victorious formula course, we will have less protection.

We make the Foundation of Faith and the Foundation of Substance through this process. We should reclaim our original value by passing through the levels of formation, growth and completion, the Old Testament, New Testament and Completed Testament ages/word and the eight vertical levels.

What is the formula course? The formula course is everything that is written in the second part of the Divine Principle. The courses in the families of Adam, Noah, Abraham, Moses and Jesus are the explanation of the formula course that we have to follow and not just Bible stories. These parts are to explain exactly where there is focus on the human portion of responsibility in the Formula Course. That is why, at the end of the course of each family, the Divine Principle explains the lessons learned from that family. The courses of the families are explained based on the work of God seeking to establish the Foundation of Faith and the Foundation of Substance.

Going through the courses of the families does not mean that we literally need to repeat everything they did; for example, we will not need to travel through the desert like Moses did. Going through the course of the families means that the essence of what they experienced will be repeated in our life or in the life of our family. In a similar way to what Moses had to do, a central figure takes care of many people (spiritual children, members of the Home Group) and guides them to want to create the Kingdom of Heaven, but they always claim they want to crucify the central figure. Similar situations such as these may occur within our formula course and each moment has something internal about it to restore the heart of God.

God called Noah to build the ark, not near the sea, but at the top of the mountain. In our formula course we do not need to build an ark literally, but we can receive a similar test of faith similar, for example, the central figure asks us to do something that from a logical point of view is difficult to believe in.

In the case of the Adam's family the test was the problem of Adam and Eve and the problem of Cain and Abel. These tests also occur within our formula course. If we repeat the same mistakes (sin) of the past, this will increase the indemnity which has to be paid, but if we go the reverse way in accordance with the Will of God, practising the opposite of what happened in the past, we are restoring the past through indemnity. To complete the work of restoration through indemnity it is not possible by only having faith but also requires that invest ourselves through some action in a particular situation.

We can restore ourselves through this formula course. Through this process of laying a Foundation of Faith and Foundation of Substance, we can raise our spirituality, passing through the period of training, growing up to the level of perfection of the growth period (prior to receiving the Blessing). We must mature our love to the level that Adam reached at the age of 14 - 16 years. The sum total of our individual formula course is to reach the level of perfection of the growth stage.

Jesus said that we must be like children otherwise we cannot enter the Kingdom of Heaven. Our Father explained what Jesus meant. Inside the mother's womb the baby has no concepts of the "I" and "sex". It has no awareness of its own existence so there is no selfish-selfishness; it is a situation of zero selfishness. We must eliminate all fallen nature through the Cain and Abel relationship. Also the baby in the womb has no idea of gender and does not know what gender it is which is a situation of maximum purity in relationship between Adam and Eve. For rebirth we need to get back in the uterus by denying this life which began wrongly. Entering the uterus means being ready for rebirth, purifying ourselves completely up to the zero point of having no fallen nature or sin. If we do happen to go through this course of complete purification through denial of selfishness, but avoiding the process of the formula course, at the time we go through the process of rebirth, we will be missing internal conditions. One of the reasons why sometimes problems occur in a family after the blessing, despite doing many activities, is because the husband and wife have not been focusing on achieving victory in the formula course.

Negating our false 'I', we can discover our true self. If we eliminate our fallen nature and also our individual, collective and hereditary sins, there will be only the Original Sin left in us. Restoring the original heart of children and brothers/sisters within the Four Great Realms of Heart, we will arrive in the same situation that Adam and Eve were in immediately after the Fall. When our spirituality reaches this level we will be ready at that time to receive the blessing. What is the best preparation to receive the Blessing? Sometimes young people may think that not having fallen is already the necessary preparation to receive the blessing. This is a huge misunderstanding. Not to fall is a minimum condition for not losing the right to receive the Blessing. Then, what is the true preparation to receive the blessing? It is go through all of the stages of the formula course, growing our love and eliminating fallen nature and sin until our spirituality achieves the level of perfection of the level of the growth stage.

After we finish the individual formula course, we must then go through the process of rebirth by receiving the Blessing. Through the "uterus" of restored Eve who is True Mother, we can return to the "marrow" of the True Father and receive the seed of life, then return to the uterus of the original Eve of True Mother and be reborn.

Entering the uterus means performing a profound union of heart with True Mother. Then we need to receive the seed. The origin of the seed (sperm) is the column and spinal cord. We must enter into the spinal cord; this means that we need to make a profound union with the True Heart of True Father. Experiencing the love of True Parents and God is what make rebirth occur. In the case of the first generation, the wife is reborn first, standing in the position of daughter in relationship to our Father, while the husband remains in the position of archangel,.

The wife has to be born again first. During the first period of separation of 40 days before starting family life the wife must first experience the heart of bride and then the heart of wife before our True Father. She later remains in the position of mother and our True Father in the position of father and together they can give rebirth to the archangel (husband).

The separation period of 40 days is not simply a period to wait for permission to begin family life. It is a time to restore the original heart. This is very important. If you have not restored, step by step, the heart of our Father, although you started family and have older children aged 15 or 20 years old you must, starting now, restore that heart.

When do you finish the formula course? When you have restored what needs to be restored. You are not just restoring the formula course. When you go to the spiritual world, you will discover inside of yourself those contents/conditions which were not restored on earth.

Fulfilment of the formula course is not a question of the size of your dedication, time doing activities or sacrifice in the church; the essence of the formula course is the perfection of love. Activities, sacrifice and dedication are ways to restore love. The question is whether or not we have restored what should be restored. Whether we sacrificed only very little or sacrificed very much, if we have not restored love, we will have to continue our restoration. There may even be situations where, after making many sacrifices, a person increases their resentment instead of increasing their love. In this case they will be avoiding the formula course. Concerning the formula course our 7 years, our Father stated that even if we are not restored and did not come to individual perfection within 7 years, we must continue to work to achieve it. On the other hand, if you already restored everything that you need to restore before the end of 7 years, and completed the formula course, it is only a matter of waiting to move up to completion of the number 7.

In our life of faith the internal system for members is optional but the course followed is not. Although the system of internal member was formed the formula course continues. Understanding only the external aspect of the activities a person may think that they are helping the church, but when understood more deeply about the fact that we are sinners and need an internal formula course, we come to understand that it is the church that is helping us, giving us opportunities to walk the formula course.

It is better to think that God and True Parents are helping us stay here, since as sinners we are not worthy. Before thinking about how such or such an activity helped the Church, it is better to think that God, who forgives us, is allowing us to make amends. When we understand deeply the fact that we are sinners our vision can become external and make it easier for us to become arrogant. If we become more arrogance it means that we are not fulfilling the formula course.

Returning to the matter of the process of rebirth, if we did not restore our heart towards True Father perfectly (the heart of the daughter, wife, mother), but still do everything in an official manner in accordance with the guidance of the Blessed Family Department, Original Sin will still be removed and we will give birth to children of the Second Generation without Original Sin. But, when we compare the case of those who have restored all the contents of the formula course before the Blessing including the heart that we must restore in the course of separation and the other case of those that did not restore, there is certainly an internal difference.

During the formula course, restoration of the heart in each stage only occurs through actual experience and is not something vague, like for example: "one only has to believe".

After the 3 day ceremony, after completion of all conditions, by joining as a couple we can create children of the Second Generation. The Second Generation is in the position of Abel and our spiritual children in the position of Cain.

The education and seminars that we provide for our young people of the Second Generation are very important. But, beyond that, it is also very important that parents successfully restored many spiritual children victoriously with love and sacrifice even to the point where they say voluntarily and with joy: "*Thank you so much for your love and effort to restore us. Now we want to help in the growth of your Second Generation children. We will assume responsibility for their care and educate them until they receive the blessing*". The spiritual father should receive these words as a result of having naturally subjugated his spiritual children during completion of the conditions in the formula course.

In the formula course the spiritual children must wait with joy for the birth of the Second Generation, and the original archangels and, after the birth, must care for and educate them until they receive the Blessing. The Third Generation will then be born and receive the Blessing.

If we do not achieve success in witnessing, without having won over Cain in the individual formula, when passing through the course of spiritual rebirth, there will internal conditions missing and also we will not have much status in spiritual protection for the Second Generation.

Any victory that is missing in the individual formula course will appear as an effect in the Blessing. Although a person is doing activities, if they did not achieve real victory in the formula course for example failing to end fights between Cain and Abel or continuing to express fallen nature, the same test is going to happen in their family life.

The formula course must be something universal and is for all human beings. We must understand the difference between external activities and the formula course. Material restoration through selling pencils or other fundraising products is not an essential part of the formula course. There were no pencils or money at the time of Adam and Eve.

If we understand the essence of the formula course, although we change our mission and activity, we can continue the formula course. If we do not understand these things well enough, although we are performing many activities externally, it may be that these activities are not operating as part of the formula course.

After passing through the stages mentioned above, to the original position of Adam, that allow us to remove the Original Sin, we must then do activities to restore our homeland as a Tribal Messiah. Restoring our tribe (Abel type) and other spiritual children (Cain type), we must achieve the restoration of 430 families.

Then we must restore the conditions for the First and Second Blessing, restore the right of parents; establish material conditions in the tribe as a type of Third Blessing; complete the growth our the heart as a spouse and parent within the Four Great Realms of Heart; fulfil the Three Blessings and restore the right of Kingship, the three Great Kingships and the Realm of the Royal Family. By adding all of these we make the condition for the registration for heaven, in which we are citizens of Cheon Il Guk. We will go into the level of Direct Dominion of God.

In future, when restoring the Kingdom of Heaven, there will be substantial registration for the Kingdom of Heaven. The queue made to register as citizens of the Kingdom of Heaven will be the longest row ever seen in human history, because all human beings should register themselves. There will be a table with the items to fill in, such as full name, address, telephone number, date of birth, etc., but the most important items for the record will be our victory as a Tribal Messiah. We will not be permitted to register without this condition.

Tribal Messiah is the name of the condition for entering the Kingdom of Heaven. Tribal Messiah is the formula course. Through our activity as a Tribal Messiah we can pass all of the contents of the formula course.

The internal membership system is good for learning the essence of the formula course and after that learning to help master the mission of Tribal Messiah. But if one is only focused on the completion of external activities and does not understand the essence, then we will be lost when we start activities as a Tribal Messiah, without understanding the contents that should be restored on each level.

The formula course is the process of becoming a mature adult in the Kingdom of Heaven. While becoming adult is not optional, the perfection and the individual formula course are also not optional.

Individual perfection does not mean that man will become perfect simply like a machine, but rather, it means making the minimum condition needed to be able to live as an adult in the Kingdom of Heaven. Just as in the case of car working well, and someone only being able to travel freely in it after all the operational functions are in order, such as the tyres, lights, accelerator, brakes and so on, then Man must also have the condition to operate perfectly, including fulfilling the conditions of the Four Great Realms of the Heart (heart of the child, sibling, spouse and parents) and then one can increase the joy of True Love forever. Individual perfection is not the end point of the purpose and creativity of the human being, becoming a monotonous routine. In fact it is the opposite, just the beginning, where Man will be free to enjoy true freedom, true love and original creativity.

Because he is dominated by fallen nature, a fallen person always acts in the same manner in situations in life. For example, such a person always becomes irritated if someone speaks about a certain thing. Or, in the context of an intimate relationship, always reaches the limit of his emotions and starts to fight when similar situations occur, time and time again etc. Satan and evil spirits know our weaknesses well and touch these points every time an opportunity arises. Then they use this condition in which we demonstrated fallen nature to overpower us. We can sometimes be still dominated by the same fallen natures for more than 10 years without getting out of the dominion of Satan and evil spirits. Even though if we are doing many activities in the church and even bringing significant results in the providence, if we do not focus on resolving this point we can remain for many years without resolving this problem.

In the book from Dr. Sang Hun Lee[1] it is written that a spirit who participated in the Divine Principle seminar stated that, if the whole world were to become perfect, the world would

[1] A list of Dr. Lee's publications can be found at http://www.unification.net/leesanghun/

not be interesting because everyone would be equal. Dr. Sang Hun Lee explained that this is very wrong. In truth it is just the opposite. The fallen world is not interesting because everyone has the same reaction in the same situations when they are touched by the emotions arising from fallen nature. On the other hand, if the entire world is released from fallen nature and sin, the original nature of each would be freed, as well as the gift for writing poems, the gift for creating music, the gift for creating to literature etc. and the world would become very interesting.

The world where fallen nature dominates has no freedom of the Original Mind since it is under the bondage of Satan.

The words of our Father say that: *everyone, no matter who they are, has to pass through the formula course. People who are proud and different. Ugly and unfortunate people, no matter who they are: all have to go through this course. Any person who is the offspring of the Fall has to go through this course, not matter who he or she is, otherwise they can never enter the Kingdom of Heaven.* (Blessing and Ideal Family II).

This is the formula for all human beings. The formula course has this feature: it does not matter whether we know it or not, whether we accept it or not, the fact is that every human being has to pass beyond the will or desire not to move forward. If we reject this on earth, we must continue the process in the spiritual world.

The ideal of a blessed family should not be simply: "I know that our Father is the Messiah, I received the blessing, I am not going to fall, I have a home, employment, health, etc." The ideal of the blessed family is something much more specific: "Realization of the Three Great Blessings, individual perfection, marriage, the Four Great Realms of Heart, elimination of all fallen nature, removal of sin, liberation of ancestors, then registering to enter heaven, becoming a citizen of the Cheon Il Guk, the Kingdom of Heaven. We do Home Group activities to go through the formula course. We cannot have proper Home Groups without understanding the contents of the formula course.

Perfecting the relationship of Cain and Abel is only part of the formula course. After completion of the individual course we receive the blessing and then we are to restore the homeland as a Tribal Messiah. That is why we must overcome the Cain and Abel challenge as quickly as possible. If you are continuously repeating the fight between Cain and Abel, you will stay at the level of the Growth Stage and lack any condition to register for and receive the blessing.

If we still have Cain and Abel conflicts it means that we have not yet developed the heart of "parents". Without experiencing victory as Cain and Abel we will not reach the heart of "parents" in any true meaning. Messiah is "parents". That is why Tribal Messiah is "parents". If we do not have the heart of parents we will only be defeated in the mission of Tribal Messiah.

The Tribal Messiah

To be a Tribal Messiah ....

1. is to love our tribe with the same heart that we love the family and tribe of Our Father because he can't love them directly at that time.

2. is to inherit the love and the heart of True Parents, experiencing, at our level, the same path that he trod.
3. is a condition for liberating the ancestors.
4. is to reach the direct dominion of God through the 8 vertical and horizontal levels that our Father walked, taking advantage of the great concession given by him.
5. is to substantially transform our homeland into the Kingdom of Heaven, not only to restore spiritual children. To transform your homeland into the Kingdom of Heaven, is the eternal mission of a Tribal Messiah.
6. is to walk the formula course as a way of "absolute destination".

Eight Vertical Levels and Eight Horizontal Levels

The eight vertical levels are: servant of servants, servant, adopted child, illegitimate child (step-child), child, mother, father, God and the eight horizontal levels are: individual, family, tribe, race, nation, world, cosmos and God.

Our Father completed this journey of eight vertical and horizontal levels, overcoming all sorts of Cain and Abel issues, restoring the right of inheritance (birthright). Since our Father completed this, it became the formula course for all human beings.

After our Father achieved victory, there was a meeting between God, Our Father and Satan. Our Father, who spoke to God: "Heavenly Father as I achieved victory, subjugating Satan naturally, allow me to reduce the price, so that every human being need only achieve the first three levels of individual, family and tribe, if they make it that far, I really want to give the rest to my children, as a legacy from father". God was very happy. Thus he made the conditions and it became possible for humankind to reach the direct dominion of God.

Later, our Father spoke to Satan: "Since I have achieved the victory, I am going to lower the price for humankind, after subjugating Satan naturally on the cosmic level he can do nothing". Then, Satan accepted the condition. Our Father declared the era of Tribal Messiah. Since then, there have been two options for humankind to be perfected and enter the direct dominion of God. The first option is to make all the eight horizontal and vertical levels by himself, literally by repeating the course that our Father made. The other option is to become a tribal messiah and receive the inheritance of the victory of True Parents.

Tribal Messiah is the way to enter the Kingdom of Heaven and the entire world must do so. If we do not do this while we are on earth, our descendants will have to do so.

Our True Father uses the expressions "common destiny" and "absolute destiny". "Common destiny" is a destination that in practice is possible to change. For example, with marriage, in fact it is not good to separate, but it is possible that a breakup can happen in practice. "Absolute destiny" is different, for example, the relationship between parent and child. Once a person is born from his father and his mother it is impossible to change that reality, even God is not able to change the fact of being a father and mother of someone. Absolutely nobody can change this reality. That is why it is called "absolute destiny".

Our Father, using this expression, placed great emphasis on being a tribal messiah. He said that the mission of the Tribal Messiah is an "absolute destiny"

The Formula Course from Various Viewpoints

In the original world we would need to go through formation, growth and completion to reach the direct dominion of God, 7 years, 7 years, and 7 years. In the process of restoration however, we must go from hell, to Old Testament, New Testament and Completed Testament, 2000, 2000, and 2000 years. The difference between 2000 years and 7 years is huge. In the sense of the restoration of the eight vertical levels, we must go from servant of servants, servant, adopted child, illegitimate child (step-child), child, mother, father and God. In the sense of the Four Great Realms of Heart the formula course is so we can experience the heart of a child, sibling, partner, and parents. In the sense of the Three Great Blessings, we must fulfil the first blessing, the second blessing and the third blessing. In the sense of the restoration of the three rights of inheritance, we must restore the birthright of the elder son, the right of parents and the right of the king. In the sense of the foundation of the original world, we must establish the foundation of faith and the foundation of substance. In the course of the restoration, we must establish the foundation to receive the Messiah, which is the foundation of faith and the foundation of substance. This is the way to individual perfection (first blessing) followed by the second and third blessings.

The only way to complete the formula course is to complete the human portion of responsibility. In other words, this means that the human portion of responsibility is to accomplish everything that was mentioned above. It may seem very complicated when presented from several points of view, but in truth, it expresses the single formula course that is the way to enter and live in the Kingdom of Heaven.

The formula course is the path to the perfection of our love. Next, the human portion of responsibility is the growth and perfection of love. And as we saw, the concept of the human portion of responsibility is different from the common concept of the word "responsibility" used in society.

Based on the formula course, we carry out restoration activities for all physical things (e.g. fund-raising and after that we witness to restore mankind. On the foundation of these activities, reaching the perfection level of the growth stage, we receive the marriage Blessing to continue restoring the original heart to the completion stage.

Conditions to receive the Blessing were originally strict: we needed to make many conditions, such as seven days fasting, 120 days of restoring all things, exemplary behaviour, the signatures of three central figures, a minimum of 3 to 12 spiritual children, etc.

The era changed and we were given lesser conditions to receive the Blessing, but the distance between the person and purpose has not lessened. This means that, although the time is different, the level of spirituality of each one remains in the same position. And also the value of individual perfection has not dropped. That is why the journey that we have to make was not shortened because of the change of era.

Originally it was said, in order to receive the Blessing, we must grow to the level of perfection of the growth stage, developing love, eliminating all our fallen nature and all our sin, except only the original sin. But, in many cases we receive the Blessing before reaching this stage. In this case, the distance between the standard at which we can receive the Blessing and our standard becomes an accusation from Satan. The greater the distance between our spiritual standard and the standard of the level of perfection of the growth stage, the greater will be Satan's accusation and this will increase the possibility of breaking the Blessing, and not being able to handle the pressure. In the end, the best preparation to receive the Blessing is to grow in love and spirituality through the completion of the formula course. In truth, preparation to receive the Blessing is nothing else but the fact that love has grown.

Although Adam and Eve were pure, they were seduced by Satan and fell. In our case, we are at a different level from Adam and Eve. Although not reaching the level of perfection of the growth stage, our Father allowed us to receive the Blessing as if we had already achieved it. But with this, we are committed to grow as quickly as possible after the Blessing and justify the lack of conditions and standard. In this situation, before and after the Blessing, Satan can attack us with the same intensity that Adam and Eve were attacked at the level of perfection of the growth stage.

This type of testing of love that can cause the fall or the breakdown of the Blessing and can make you lose all the merit of your whole life of faith, is called "Spiritual Golgotha" or "Spiritual Calvary".

The lives of monks, nuns and priests, are not easy; those who were born outside of the time of True Parents, for example, 100 years earlier, had no opportunity to receive the Blessing. Through hard religious training and maintaining their purity, they were able to raise their spiritual standard only up to the level of perfection of the growth stage, but they ended up in a situation where they could not grow more. They had no means to climb further; they should not fall and in addition always received violent attacks from Satan. In this situation, some monks or nuns did not continue, lost the power to go on and fell. With only one night of fall, they lost all the merit that they had accumulated during their religious life. At this point, the only hope for human beings is True Parents that matured with the accomplishment of the substantial family four position foundation.

The Difference between Sin and Fallen Nature (The Way to Eliminate Fallen Nature)

The Divine Principle book defines sin as "the act of violating heavenly law by setting a condition in which you form a reciprocal basis with Satan and enter in an action of giving and receiving with him". In a tree, individual sin is compared to the leaves, collective sin to the branches, hereditary sin to the trunk and the original sin to the root. Sin is the act of violating heavenly law, then, if there is no heavenly law, there was no sin. If God did not establish the Principle of Creation which is the origin of heavenly law, there would be no sin. Sin is something contrary to the will of God. The will of God is caused by the love and heart of God.

Fallen nature is somewhat different from sin. The Divine Principle defines fallen nature in this way: "Eve inherited from the archangel all the characteristics that eventually emerged when the archangel committed a sexual act with Eve, revealing himself to be against God. Then Adam, who entered into a blood relationship with Eve, who in turn was in the position of the archangel to him, came to inherit the same essential characteristics that caused all the fallen nature of fallen men. We give to these the name of the "original nature of the fall" (fallen nature). There are four categories of fallen nature. The First is: "being unable to take the same point of view of God in loving others". Lucifer did not love Adam and Eve, in the way they were loved by God. The second is "stepping out of their own position". The Third is "reversing dominion" and the fourth is "multiplying the unlawful act".

Fallen nature and sin do not exist within the physical body. DNA does not change because of this. If sin existed within the flesh, it would be easy to go to the doctor and start again through surgery. Sin is a spiritual problem and is internal. Sin is a concept that manifests within relationships. The way to solve it is through law in the sense that in a court, God is the judge, the Messiah is the defence attorney and Satan is the prosecutor. They are also the victim and the defendant. If the judge says that he can forgive the prosecutor and the victim too, then the sin can be forgiven. If there were no God, there would be no sin. Sin is an invisible thing.

If a person commits sin, Satan wins the right to attack him. This right is called a "condition of accusation from Satan". This condition of accusation is invisible, but when Satan carries out his work, claiming and using his right, this appears as a substantial action on the earth through the actions of people. Satan makes reciprocal relationships of giving and receiving action with the spirits of people on the earth, which in turn, influences them to do physical action. The activities of Satan can appear physically in human society. Then, the law of Satan is invisible but his work can be manifested as a reality on earth. When a person has sin, Satan can attack him in several ways using his right, but when a person removes this sin through the establishment of an indemnity condition, God can protect him. In his situation, even though Satan has power, through lack of the condition to accuse, he does not manage to carry out his deeds. In this way, the historic providential war has been a struggle between God and Satan, centring on the question of who has or does not have the invisible "right". Although God has power, if lacking the right, he cannot act. In the case of Satan, it is the same thing, although Satan has the power, he cannot act if he does not have the right. Mankind is in the mid-way position between God and Satan. God and Satan are fighting centring on the human portion of responsibility. "Indemnity conditions" are the human portion of responsibility.

The way to get rid of sin is to establish a "condition of indemnity" equivalent in size to the "condition of accusation" that appeared when the sin was committed. After doing this, Satan loses the right (the condition) to accuse.

Fallen nature is different, because it is a question of habit. Although a person resolves his sin, the habit can still remain within. For example, a man goes to prison because of his crime, after paying the penalty to society, his debt is settled, but his habit leading to him committing such a crime still didn't leave him. When such a person comes out of prison, he can go on to commit the same sin (offence) again. Once fallen nature has become a matter of habit, the way to resolve it is different from the way to resolve sin. Fallen nature is only resolved through the discipline of practising. It is only settled by correcting the habit through practising and investing in each action whenever fallen nature is manifested.

Drinking the Holy Wine, removes original sin, but is it possible for it to eliminate fallen nature? Could it be that unconsciously, walking down the street, people's fallen nature can come off and fall on the floor? It's not like that at all. Only when you are consciously striving are you going to eliminate fallen nature. Without effort and without training, whatever a person's age—10, 20, 30 or 100 years, fallen nature will not simply disappear. Such is the severity of man's fallen state. All pastors say in their prayers that it is no use to accumulate wealth on earth, like houses, money, cars, etc. because you will not be able to take them to heaven). We say something similar, but in the opposite sense: there is something that you don't want to take with you to the spiritual world in any form and even you try to stop it completely saying, quit and do not hold on to me, I don't want you here with me. When I get there, it will come back saying good morning, we arrived! What escorts you to the spiritual world? They are your fallen natures!

While a person is still on the earth it is easy to eliminate fallen nature, because he has a physical body with which to send vitality elements to the spirit. In the spiritual world is very difficult to change our habits, because the process of "understanding" is very slow. The person remains at the same level of mentality and spiritual level that was reached when on earth. Swedenborg recounts the scene of an angel trying to educate a spirit person who practised free sex during his life on earth. The angel explained that free sex is a bad thing, it is sin, you are not allowed to do it, but the spirit did not understand even when the angel repeated it 100 or 1000 times. In this case, the only way to resolve it is to cooperate with the descendants through their actions producing vitality elements on earth. This spirit would receive benefits, and by growing together would change their spirituality. Otherwise you can never remove your fallen nature.

Many evil spirits are in hell and for many years have refused to apologize, because they don't have enough courage to do so. On Earth, while still having a physical body, although difficult, it is many times easier than in the spiritual world. In the spiritual world it becomes almost impossible to speak even one word that is not your custom. If by chance they were to speak only once, it would be possible to leave that situation in hell, but they fail to do so for years and years. That leads to the expression "eternal fire". The issue of habit is very serious.

In the next section we are going to see concrete examples of fallen nature. This is the main tool of the Home Group. We use this to set the "Weekly Goal".

Table: Fallen Nature 1
Not taking God's point of view.

<table>
<tr><td>Selfishness</td><td>Jealousy
Envy</td><td>Suspicion
Mistrust</td><td>Hatred
Resentment
Loathing
Aversion</td><td>Attempted murder</td></tr>
<tr><td colspan="3">Breaking relationships
Conceit
Self Satisfaction
Vanity
Isolation
Slander
Apathy
Irony
Antipathy</td><td colspan="2">You are unable to feel joy with the happiness of others.
Pleasure in the unhappiness of others.
Has a narrow vision
Exclusion.
Nepotism.</td></tr>
</table>

Decreased Love
You are unable to take the same position or see the situation of God.
You cannot see with the same heart as God. (Relationship between father and son)
You are unable to love with the heart of God.
You cannot love the things (people) that God loves.
You love only the things (people) that you like.
Selfishness
Love (Love enemy)
Love from the point of view of God.
Love with the heart of God.
Love with the heart of the Father (Mother)

Find the vertical relationship with God. (Prayer)
Overcome the feeling of "love rejected".
Love the enemy.
Feel the heart of True Parents in oneself.

For a person who identifies that type of fallen nature, the solution is to do the opposite. When someone fails to love from the same view point as God, they must strive to love. This is already training for individual perfection. The definition of "individual perfection" explains that we have to love in the same way that God loves. If you are feeling the same things as God, it becomes easy to overcome the feeling of decreased love and you can love any type of enemy. This is training for the individual perfection: increase your love and remove your fallen nature.

Table: Fallen Nature 2
Leaving One's Proper Position.

<table>
<tr><td>Desire for adultery
Fornication
Lust
Rage
Fury
Wrath</td><td>Hysteria
Excessive Irritability
Excessive Nervous-
ness
Uncontrolled Fury
Impatience
Sorrow
Unreliability</td><td>Demanding
Complaining
Insulting
Backbiting
Dissatisfaction
Regret
Excessive desire
Greed</td><td>Rudeness
Vulgarity
Infidelity
Seduction
Betrayal
Flirting
Capriciousness
"Disoriented"
Flattery</td></tr>
<tr><td colspan="4">Confused between public interest with individual interest.
Failure to comply with their obligations.
Irresponsibility
Moral Inability
Makes the body weak
Laziness
Escapes from Reality</td></tr>
</table>

Becoming Lost

Receive love and the word (= direction) through Abel as a mediator.

Table: Fallen Nature 3
Reversal of Dominion

Arrogance Vanity Boastfulness Pretentiousness Showing off	Stubbornness Bad temper Privately whingeing Inferiority Complex A superiority complex You are unable to be: pure/natural/simple/frank/honest.
Critical False Accusation Accusatory Insincere Flattering	You cannot obey what is to be obeyed. You don't hear the words (opinions) of others. "The intention" and "the way of communicating" are confused and not differentiated.
Repulsion Rejection Insurrection Rebellion Resistance Threat	Tries to feel happiness by attributing "fallen love" to the other.

Loses the proper relationship.
Destroys order and causes confusion.

Put oneself in the position to obey to Abel (= Central figure) and be under his dominion.

The person who has this fallen nature tends to dislike obeying another person. And for that person religious training and the discipline of obedience is very good to correct this fallen nature. In such cases, the amount of fallen nature is equivalent in size to the degree of conflict that the person will feel. But once it runs out, the benefit he receives in changing his life will be equivalent to the size of the conflict that he overcame.

Table: Fallen Nature 4
Multiplication of Sin

<table>
<tr><td colspan="2">Shift the blame to another.
You are unable to reflect.
You are unable to repent.
Self-justification
Evasion
Makes crafty excuses
Subterfuge
Self - limitation</td><td colspan="2">Pride
Is only concerned with his appearance to others.
Lies
Rumours
Hides
Does not match his "Words" with "Action"</td></tr>
<tr><td>Lack of Seriousness
Contempt
Does not take anything seriously.</td><td colspan="2">Relaxed
Negligent
Carefree
Lack of commitment
Discouragement
Vagrancy</td><td>Lack of firmness
Blend in
Be content
Comply with
Corporatism</td></tr>
<tr><td>You cannot forgive.
Hold grudges.</td><td colspan="2">Persecution Complex
Feel despised.</td><td>Complicity
Speaking ill of the others behind their backs.</td></tr>
</table>

You unable to accept responsibility for yourself.
You want to avoid responsibility.
Attribute blame to others and to the circumstances.

Multiplying Goodness

With this category of fallen nature, we must analyse ourselves and repent. Because this particular content, based on the Divine Principle is sharp as a sword, we should not use it to criticize and analyse each other. If most of the expressions of fallen nature are being practised by the mouth, then, if we can control our words, a large part of our fallen nature will be controlled. This is the first step. We must monitor ourselves.

Practical Ways to Remove Fallen Nature

As was said before, the way to resolve fallen nature is to correct our habits through the practice of reversing each action when the fallen nature is manifested.

Before discussing this topic specifically, we are going to explain a particular part of the Divine Principle: "Good or evil in the conduct of man brings a physical influence to the spiritual man, to render it good or bad. The reason is that the physical man supplies a particular element to the spiritual man (vitality element). In our daily lives, we know that our mind is happy when our body performs some good action, but feels anguish after bad conduct. The reason is that the vitality element introduced to our spiritual man can be good or bad according to the actions of the physical man.

Whenever a person does something good with his physical body, it sends vitality elements to purify his spirit and change his habits. If you perform bad actions, you send bad elements to the spirit. "The spirit man can only grow and be purified on the foundation of the physical man".

To change the spirit it is necessary to make substantial conditions of action with the physical body in order to send vitality elements to the spirit. Sometimes we feel that we are normal people, good people, but as every human being is fallen, fallen nature exists within each of us. Fallen nature prevents our individual perfection makes it impossible for us to receive and freely share the love of God. Fallen nature interferes with our relationships with the people we love, our spouse, children, friends etc. Those people who are closest to us such as our spouse, children, friends and relatives can feel like enemies more easily, because they are more precious to us. This happens when we feel even a little dissatisfied in love with the relationships with these people, and we become very disappointed.

Fallen man is living in a miserable situation for not understanding fallen nature. First, by not managing to control it, he performs the fallen nature, then gets frustrated because of his actions and then forgets and proceeds to practice it again, repeating the whole process. When a fallen emotion appears, all fallen people act in the same manner. In this state of affairs, in reality, mankind has no freedom (freedom of the original mind).

Fallen nature accompanies us for a long time and will accompany us into the spiritual world if we do not resolve it. In this sense, our life of faith only really begins when we discover and consciously decided to fight against this problem. By learning how to remove fallen nature we can improve our personal relationship with God, our relationships within the family and with other people. Fallen nature is what prevents us from achieving and living in a state of individual perfection.

In the Home Groups we have an opportunity to confront our fallen natures and overcome them through the "Weekly Goal". Different to sin, fallen nature is not eliminated only by conditions and just receiving the forgiveness of God. To remove fallen nature we must make conscious actions.

While we have a physical body, we have a valuable opportunity to remove our fallen nature, because we can produce "vitality elements" by ourselves which will improve our spirit selves. In order to remove fallen nature we must practise "even against our will". For example, imagine that a husband is determined not to fight and not to be angry with his wife in the difficult moments when they reach the limits of their emotion. One day, he feels very irritated because of some situation and almost wants to fight. At that time, acting against the will of his fallen nature, he smiles and acts naturally as if not irritated, saying kind words in a positive way. The wife may accuse him by saying that he is still false, acting differently from what he is feeling inside. If at that time he gives up, he will lose all of the mer-merit accumulated until then, but if he keeps going to the end, there will be an internal change. In this way, he will continue to grow until reaching a level of spirituality where such types of test are no longer needed. This is what is meant by "practising, even against your will". If you focus on the fight against your own fallen nature, you can avoid fights with others and be able to discover that in reality that falseness is the fallen nature inside yourself.

When we are tested in our relationships with other people, it is a good opportunity to fight against our own fallen nature. Regardless of who is right or wrong, if we deny ourselves because of our love for others, we can discover a "new me". Only in this moment we will be denying the "false me" to liberate the original mind. The same level at which we get rid of our fallen nature is the same level at which we liberate the original mind. Very often, we forget the fact that we need to increase the amount love inside ourselves whenever we question "who is right or wrong" and then we lose the chance to defeat the fallen nature inside us. In Home Group activities we emphasise that "My love must overcome my fallen nature"!

An indemnity condition (jeongseong) on its own is not enough to change a person's state within a certain time period. Let's say a person externally fulfils an indemnity condition of 40 minutes during 21 days and immediately claims to be victorious. But, internally it may be different. For example, for some of those days the person made the condition with enough faith and love to achieve the purpose (example: win a spiritual son), but on other days he lost hope and made the condition almost asleep, without much faith. In this case the internal quality of the condition was unstable. This is one of the reasons why sometimes, even though a person makes many conditions, he does not have witnessing results. It is not that he was not making conditions, but that he was not maintaining the degree of faith and love required.

If you meet a condition of indemnity in accordance with the will of God, He can accept it and do His work using such a condition. But, if you fail, Satan will be qualified to accuse to the same degree and will be able to do his work using such condition of accusation.

For real changes to occur in our life we have to acquire the status of people with substantial achievement. Indemnity conditions such as, for example, prayer, worship etc. function to establish conditions for the foundation of faith, but, if conditions are lacking in the form of substantial "practice", we will not be able to complete the process of real change in our lives. This "practice" is to substantially remove the habits of fallen nature by sending vitality elements and change the level of spirituality.

When we determine to fight against fallen nature, we must take account of this reality.

In the effort (practise) towards a goal, there is a concept that considers substantial action itself to be a condition.

When we do more prayer, we gain more spiritual strength to take action and when we overcome by doing the action, this will facilitate the prayer. Doing these two types of conditions ("indemnity condition" and "goal of effort - action"), we will increase our spiritual strength to overcome our fallen nature.

In some cases we do many conditions through prayer, fasting, etc., but do not notice that the part that completes the condition through personal substantial action, is missing and therefore the problem is not resolved or we don't get results in witnessing.

If we invest heavily in prayer, a second before displaying fallen nature, we will remember the goal of the condition and it can be controlled. Without the support of prayer it will not be easy to dominate our own fallen nature at the most crucial moments. It is therefore very important to set the external goal, together with the prayer condition.

Example -1- On the Indemnity Condition

This goal can be for the improvement of a couple's relationship, between parents and children, Cain and Abel or it may be to remove any fallen nature or for growth of the original heart. When fallen nature is hidden, it does not mean that the person does not have fallen nature. When fallen nature manifests itself, there is a good opportunity to eliminate it. If conflicts do not appear to bring out fallen nature, you will not be able to eradicate it.

Example -2- On the Indemnity Condition and the External Goal

In the external goal, you can make two goals, one for doing something and another not to do something, and it is also better that the husband and wife begin the condition together, because one is going to remind the other and the result will be effective. In order to facilitate the action it is better to make the external goal as concrete as possible.

If you don't reveal your original heart, you will not look at your spouse with the eyes of God and to discover beauty in your partner.

Example -3- On the Indemnity Condition and the Goal of these Activities

Here are some practical examples from members who managed to improve their couple's relationship.

> *"When we started to fight against our fallen nature the stronger our determination, the more we felt the reaction of our fallen nature. Similar to the process of chemical detoxification, fallen nature is deeply rooted in us and does not come out easily. During this process, we felt as if we were going to kill each other, therefore, as fallen people, we are hypnotized by our fallen nature. In the beginning we struggled to control our fallen nature (it was difficult), but later the need to control it is less (it is easy), because the desire to act on our fallen nature didn't appear."*

Within the Home Group there are opportunities to do this.

When a couple sets an external goal of no fighting, during the time period stated, the exact circumstances of that specific issue (fighting between the couple) will manifest, because God and Satan both know the human portion of responsibility, is necessary for the fulfilment of this "goal" and to decide who shall have the right to claim this couple.

Tests in school come through a sheet of paper, but tests in the life of faith are not through paper but come in the form of real situations of relationships between people. When shown the evidence, the focus is whether the person wins or fails in the declared "goal". For each test there is always God's desire that he wants his child to overcome the challenge. For example, "in this test, you must win, overcoming fallen love" or "in this test you must overcome, loving the enemy until the end", etc. Then, we must discover the focus of the will of God in each case, in each test. In this situation, the victory does not depend on the details of the case, but more on achieving the "goal" (human portion of responsibility).

As soon as you are inside the time period of the external goal, you should show a perfect standard of practice in each of the tests that will appear, until the end of the time period. Only when you do this, will you accumulate sufficient condition to cause real change. In this period, if you fail once, you will remain at the same level of spirituality, you will lose all of the conditions established so far and will need to establish the same condition ("goal") once more.

If you achieve the "Weekly Goal" beating all the challenges that occur in this period, this will set the necessary condition to cause spiritual growth up to the level that there will be no more fights between the couple of the same type and degree of the condition. Once that has been surpassed, if by chance the same test happens again, it will no longer irritate the person, because you've already substantially overcome that difficulty by increasing the capacity your love.

By repeating this process to overcome the challenge, anger rising spiritually and the number of fights between the couple will decrease and they can even reach zero. But if they fight and fail, giving up completely, the next condition will begin at the same level as before.

It is not good to leave a period of time between one condition and another; it will not solve the problems of fallen nature if we take an interval to bring out our fallen nature between one external goal period and another.

In the Home Groups we practise the "Weekly Goal" based on this part of the Divine Principle.

Chapter 2.
Overview of the Home Groups Method

There are two very important points that we need to understand to achieve success in the Home Groups providence.

The first is that success not only depends on the practical effort we make, but rather depends on how much we gain a clear and precise understanding of the essence and purpose of Home Groups. That's why we will be working hard to develop good materials for Home Group study, for example, a series of good quality, themed study sessions, a DVD of the seminars explaining the vision of Home Groups, this manual, a website and collecting testimonies from Home Group members. Building on these materials, we will go with confidence in raising our understanding and consequently the development of Home Groups throughout the nation and thus support the victory of Vision 2020.

The second point is that our primary concern in the providence of Home Groups should not be predominantly focussed on external achievement. On the contrary, it must be internal, towards oneself. First you must search for and should find an internal victory. Our principal focus of a Home Group is not to start mobilizations or find people to send to seminars. We need to have a clearly directed mind to seek internal victory before anything else.

Before we start worrying about testifying to our Home Group guests we need to become heavenly people within the Home Group in order to develop our hearts and love. What if we were to discover that are unable to love one or two families within the Home Group, how can we hope to enter into the Kingdom of Heaven? Before we aspire to enter into the Kingdom of Heaven, we need to care about loving those people who are closest to us, within the Home Group. The Home Group is a training place to become citizens of Cheon Il Guk.

The first focus of the Home Group is not to witness, but is to make the Kingdom of Heaven within ourselves. The Home Group is meant to bear witness, but the first focus is not witnessing.

The initial goal of the Home Group is to live the experience of the Kingdom of Heaven. Successful testimony will be a natural result of my experience of the Kingdom of Heaven.

In the Kingdom of Heaven there is love, heart and multiplication of goodness. Likewise, it does not have any judgment, hatred, resentment or multiplication of evil. To become citizens of Cheon Il Guk we have to be people who can live lives of goodness: Without multiplication of evil, hatred, resentment, etc., and to do this, we need some training. This was the reason why, in the internal guidance part of this manual, we learned about the fallen natures, sins and how to resolve them.

When forming a small group, if I cannot love the person sitting next to me, I cannot enter the Kingdom of Heaven. The main activity of the Home Group is to become familiar with the experience of the Kingdom of Heaven. The Home Group exists for my individual perfection through the Formula Course. The Home Group will become interesting when we reach victory in the growth of love. We participate in the Home Group while taking our individual perfection seriously, believing that it is completely possible to reach.

Home Group Anatomy and Differences between the Local and Regional Systems

Home Group Anatomy

The Home Groups are like cells of a body and the greater church (where there is an official central figure) is the brain. The Church (FFWPU) and the Home Groups must operate as a fully united organic body. There is a single centre (the brain) that is the greater Church. But the cells can multiply infinitely. Although the number of cells can increase greatly, all obey the directions of a single brain.

Difference between Regional Divisions and Home Groups

Regional Divisions: When the number of people has increased, it is difficult to look after them all. Then the leader must decide to divide the regions and place a representative in each region. They are representatives but only have the function of supporting the activities of the local church; they don't have any function of a small church. The speed of multiplication is slower and does not effectively increase the number of new sub-leaders.

Home Groups: Using the concept of cells, each Home Group has the similar function of a small church. The number of Home Groups will be the number of sub leaders. Through multiplication, the number of sub leaders in training will increase more and more and increase the foundation rapidly, as well as the multiplication of cells.

Solitude in the Midst of the Crowd

When we only have the sermon event in the main church, the situation of "solitude in the midst of the crowd" can occur. More than anyone realises, the members don't know each other well. They go to the Sunday sermon where there are many people, and then at the end, all return to their homes and have little opportunity to increase their relationships with each other. There are cases in which we participate together in the same location, in the same church for many years and don't really know about the life and situation and our brothers and sisters or they about ours.

When we only have the Sunday sermon, another difficulty will occur in which everyone will want to talk with the one pastor after the sermon. There will be a long queue similar to a medical consultation. Each person speaks with the pastor 20, 30, 40 minutes. The last person is discouraged and doesn't want to wait. Also on the part of the pastor, it may be that he would like to speak with a specific person because he knows that person's situation, but she became discouraged because of the wait and left. This causes a difficulty for the two sides, both the member and the pastor.

But when we open the Home Groups, as a small group with a small number of people, each person may speak and be accepted. You can then give attention to each of the participants. At the Home Groups meeting, we can deepen our understanding of the heart and the life situation of other members by sharing personal stories with each other.

Why we should not establish any Home Group with more than 12 people.

If the number of people is too large, during the hour or so of discussion after the reading, we will not be able to achieve the purpose of the Home Group which is to give attention to each and all of the participants. For example, if you have 15 people, before the last person can speak even once, he will need to wait for 14 people to talk and furthermore, if each one speaks for 5 minutes, it will be a wait of 105 minutes in total. If each one wants to say something again.... Some people would have no opportunity to express themselves freely, returning to the same situation, and the same problem as in the large church. New guests wish to speak, but do not have a lot of patience to listen for a long time.

The ideal is to begin the Home Group with about 8 people (4 couples). If you start a Home Group with a large number of people, when a guest is invited you will already need to multiply without the time to create an atmosphere of love among the members.

Through the Home Group, the atmosphere of the Sunday Sermon is transformed

When a new member goes to the Sunday Sermon event, he usually wants to be with his spiritual parent. If his spiritual parent is not present, he will be alone and feel lonely because he has no unity of heart with other people. When there are Home Groups, this situation does not occur, because the guests and new members are already familiar with all the people of the Home Group. In a Sunday Service when the spiritual parent is not present, he will feel comfortable because he knows and already has unity of heart with the members of the Home Group. This guest will find the members of the Home Group and the members will recognize him quickly and take care of him or her. All the members of the Home Group care for the spiritual children together, just as in a family. There is no concept of possession of "my" guest; rather the guest is "our" guest.

The Primary Focus for Home Groups

The Primary Focus must be Internal Victory (internal growth, change of habits, training to live a heavenly life). The main idea is not to think that the Home Group is merely a good system to increase my personal result in witnessing; rather the focus is: When we change ourselves through participating in the Home Group, this will produce a good result in witnessing. The purpose of Home Groups is to change ourselves. The main goal of the Home Groups is that each participant reaches individual perfection.

We must not think that it's only because of the system for bringing external members to Home Groups that a national witnessing explosion will occur. This national explosion will occur because of our internal unity, after the victory of love. On the other hand, even if we have internal victory, if we use a system that prevents a national explosion, for example, a linear system, the explosion will not happen. The Home Group is a system that allows an explosion of witnessing to happen.

Need for internal growth before seeing witnessing results

When we only have the greater Church (large group) Sunday Service and do not establish Home Groups (small groups), our internal growth becomes slower, since during the week we can avoid finding ourselves with people we do not have a relationship of heart with, avoiding the opportunities to overcome conflicts, to remove fallen nature and invest love for others. Usually the members are busy during the week with work and when they return home at night they have to help take care of their children. If by chance this member was not involved with church activities and did not have a concrete target for the growth of love during the week, it is possible that his spiritual growth stops. This can occur when we are not involved in caring for someone as an object of our love.

The Bible explains about the "12 pearly gates". According to True Parents' description, this means 12 different character types of people that we should love during our life on Earth (types of person A, B, C, D, E, F...). All mankind can be categorized simply into 12 types of people. In more detail, it is possible to divide each of the 12 types into 3. Then, in total there are 36 character types of people. Sometimes, we can find it easy to love a certain type of person (for example, person D, E, F). If we don't challenge ourselves to develop love towards the other types of people, when going to the spirit world, only a few gates will be open, the others remaining closed. "The gate opens" means that the person has to freely make the condition of actively giving and receiving love with that type of person. "The gate doesn't open" means that the person is not able to freely do the action of giving and receiving of love with that type of person and therefore, will feel bad and will not interact well. The activity of love becomes limited and the life of the person becomes limited.

One time, a member asked True Father which was the gate of individual perfection. Our Father put it this way: "If a person manages to have a relationship of heart with any other person, feeling so familiar although meeting for the first time because that person seems to be like some spiritual son that she loved, that person is perfect".

We are not able to personally love all people of the world, one by one, but if we love a person as representative of that type of character, it means that we can love them all. In the beginning it can be difficult, but if we work hard and break the barrier, we grow the level of love and receive love. Then, when we find someone else with that same type of character, we don't need to repeat the whole process to love that person, love will flow naturally.

Once the heart grows to certain level, with everyone below that level, a person will be able to love them immediately without effort.

If we achieve the level of perfect love to all the 12 character types of mankind, we have already reached the goal of individual perfection. In the Kingdom of Heaven we will not be lacking anything.

Witnessing is part of the formula course. Witnessing is a necessary part to complete the formula course. Without caring for (loving) a person, we cannot grow. Avoiding witnessing, we will not complete the formula course.

Through conducting tribal messiah activities, by loving 120 spiritual children, we find the way to eliminate 120 types of fallen nature. In the process of restoring 120 spiritual children, we will have 120 opportunities to grow in love. When we don't have an object of love, our mind and heart may become empty and we can even begin to criticize others. But, if we are engaged in caring for and loving several spiritual children, we will not start to criticize, because we will always be happy, feeling love. When a member does not witness, spiritual growth can stop and then the desire to complain and criticize arises. But to witness, restoring spiritual children, raises the joy of God. If you witness and do not gain spiritual children, you also continue to grow by restoring the tears of God when he lost His children. If you witness, you will resolve many things. The problem is when we remain idle.

There is no person who is fixed in the position of Cain. Each one of us is in two positions, Cain and Abel. The leader of the Home Group, for example, is in the position of Abel in caring for the members of the Home Group. All members are Abel to their spiritual children and guests. We must awaken to the two positions of Abel and Cain.

The main purpose of the Home Group is to experience the Kingdom of Heaven

With the formation of Home Groups, we can grow very quickly, because we set a specific "Weekly Goal" for internal growth. Experiencing internal growth (victory), our life of faith is more interesting and happy. The name of the goal is "Weekly Goal", but the practice should be daily. The "Weekly Goal" is the main element that will enable the Home Group to develop because it causes real changes in our lives by removing fallen nature and growing true love. The essence of the Home Group is that each member changes himself by setting and completing the "Weekly Goal".

The "Weekly Goal" is a bridge to connect the Home Group with family life

In our participation in the Home Group meeting, we must establish our "Weekly goal". From here on, every day we must remember to practise it. At the meeting in the following week, we can make an evaluation on the fulfilment of the "Weekly Goal". There is no obligation to speak publicly about the content of the goal, but all members must make one. From the point of view of the "Weekly Goal", the Home Group is not something that we practice only during the meeting, once a week, but we practice every day of the week.

Beyond making a victorious Home Group meeting, accomplishing significant union of heart between the members and guests, it is necessary to connect all that we learned in the Home Group with family life (practice within the family). If this does not occur, members may become discouraged, since they do not experience a real change in their lives by participating in the Home Group.

To avoid a disconnection between the Home Group and our family life, there is the concept of the "Weekly Goal". Through the "Weekly Goal", we can practice what we learn daily in the Home Group meeting. Struggling with our weaknesses, constantly monitoring our emotions, we can experience real changes in our lives through the Home Group. This makes the Home Group become alive and full of hope.

Without a daily victory (practice) of love, success in witnessing will not manifest

If there are conflicts between Cain and Abel within the church; this is a matter of victory of love. If there are difficulties and conflicts within couples and between parents and children in the family, this is also a question of the victory of love. These three relationships are not separate. The same fallen nature which prevents victory in the relationship between Cain and Abel in the church also prevents victory in couple's relationships and between parents and children, because, even by changing the circumstances, the same fallen nature continues within the person. If we can win in one of those relationships, this will also help us to overcome within the other relationships.

The sum of the victories of love within relationships between Cain and Abel, within couples and between parents and children will directly influence the process of acquiring spiritual children. Witnessing is also an issue of the victory of love. If there is a disconnection between our witnessing activities and our victory of love, even if we invest enough in the activities, there will be much delay in the witnessing process and its success.

In the Home Group we do not separate the victory of Cain and Abel, victory of husband and wife relationship, victory between parents and children – from the victory in witnessing. On the contrary, they all progress together. In the Home Group, we deal with these four points at the same time.

In the Home Group no one tries to change anyone else

Without changing ourselves first, trying to change others becomes impossible. If our love remains at the same level we will suffer many years trying to change, correcting, complaining or ultimately, conforming to the errors of others.

In the Home Groups activity there is a very important rule. No one tries to change anyone else. There is only one person I can try to change, that is myself. When I manage to change myself, my partner may also change. God can work freely within the Home Group and when we do not show fallen nature in the Home Group meeting we can touch the original mind and heart of each person.

How we establish a "Loving Nest"

Establishing a "Loving Nest" means that my Home Group becomes a heavenly environment, where all the members and guests can experience the Love of God flowing within each participant. If our Home Group has already created a heavenly, harmonious environment, when guests come, they will feel unity, love, etc. Then an important question is how can we create such an environment?

One of the ways to define "witnessing" is: "to bring people to meet with God and to realise the Three Great Blessings".

Based on this, the 1st type of witnessing, I can witness to myself. This means internal healing, overcoming my own internal difficulties. If we had some resentment towards God, with the church or with another member, it becomes difficult to witness to other people from outside our community. Overcoming this is the first goal of the Home Group. For us to establish a "loving nest", we need to overcome in the 1st type of witnessing.

As a 2nd type of witnessing, we must witness between ourselves (internal witnessing – between members). This means that between us we can help each other meet God and carry out the three great blessings. This will revive the members through internal unity. Only after each one removes their fallen nature and reaches the victory of love will it be possible to produce an effective unity between the members. Unity without the victory of love and without overcoming fallen nature is a limited and a superficial union. It can be shaken and ended easily and will not bring multiplication to the Home Group.

Based on the victory of the first and second kinds of witnessing, we will make the third type. This 3rd type of witnessing is for the people on the "outside" – our guests. Good results in witnessing naturally arise after we achieved victory in the 1st and 2nd kind of witnessing mentioned above.

When we achieve victory in the first and second types of witnessing, establishing good relationships, the Home Group will become a "loving nest" which will soon be able to receive guests from witnessing. We will then make the "witnessing Home Group", through the third type of witnessing, where our guests will be found.

First, we should achieve victory in the 1st and 2nd types of witnessing for multiplication to happen. But on the other hand, it should not take much, because guests can enter earlier. We want to place our guests in a loving Home Group. That is why we must focus on the first and second kinds of witnessing without losing patience. Then, we must never reject a new guest in our Home Group, although we feel that our Home Group is not yet completely harmonious. When a new guest joins the group, it means that God sent him there to further accelerate our spiritual growth. We have to accept him/her with love and gratitude and care about him becoming a child who can give joy to God.

How to develop our capacity to gain good results in witnessing?

First of all we must invest in strengthening the 1st and 2nd types of witnessing. Then within the Home Group, we can develop the ability to witness.

Including new people in Home Groups.

We must include our guests, neighbours, relatives and friends in the Home Groups. We need to "embrace" "members" and "non-members" together. Do not let the guests feel any "concept of members". If we have a "concept of members", "people of the secular world" or "people who do not know the Divine Principle", although they don't say so, they may feel some invisible barrier.

Even if a person does not want to receive testimony from the Unification Church, if she feels that in the discussion following the reading in the Home Group meeting that there is a real solution to any difficulty in her life, she will be attracted to the Home Group.

We must prepare good content for the meetings in order to attract even those guests who don't have an interest in the "Church". Here are some items that you need to have in a Home Group to attract guests in a natural way.

Have good content in the Discussion about the Reading

Have content that offers a genuine solution to the difficulties of life. For example, conflict between couples, children's education, etc., only through the Divine Principle is it truly possible to resolve problems from the very root. When we choose content for the reading, we should look for something that has to do with the real difficulties in our life (removal of fallen nature, growing in true love, couples' relationships, relationship between parents and children, etc.

Have testimonies of victory through the "Weekly Goal"

In the Home Group it is good to have testimonies about the experiences of victories through the "Weekly Goal" and encounters with the love of God and True Parents. When the guest perceives that here you have the solution for their "needs", they will become attracted by the discussion about the reading.

Let us imagine a Home Group meeting in the house of a person who has a relative living there and who is not member of the church. During the hour of reflection on the "Weekly Goal", without mentioning religious affairs, or the church, a member begins to report on the victory he is having within his family, for example, he is increasing unity and ending marital conflict, or is improving the relationship with his children, etc.

That person who is not yet a member may be going through some difficult situation related to those matters as well. He will feel interested in the Home Group because he will feel there is a possibility of real change in the actual problems of their day to day life. In this case, although he does not like religious topics, since this one discussion is exactly what he "needs" he will be attracted to the Home Group.

Real change that brings happiness to the Family

Bring real results that transform our lives.

Explanation of the Formula Course, Principles of Restoration, Four Great Realms of Heart, explanation on how to remove fallen nature, etc. is what brings solutions and real change in peoples' lives.

Establish a "loving nest" (harmonious family atmosphere) in the Home Group

Where there is love and unity, people will come!

One Home Group had an experience where they were singing a song before the meeting. Analysing externally, the song was not very nice, since it was a little off-key, even so, the neighbour who lived opposite, looked for the owner of the house the next day and told him that he felt very good listening to that song and that it was very nice. This neighbour participated in the Home Group meeting and testified that he had not experienced such a harmonious environment as that before. The people in the Home Group were working hard to create a heavenly atmosphere and loving their Home Group and that attracted the guest.

Through these four elements mentioned above, we are connecting the entire process to witnessing from within the Home Group (reading, talking about the subject, the "Weekly Goal", victory through the "Weekly Goal", real transformations in life and giving testimony to the guests). If we ignore this process and only seek results through external activities, we will not have effective results. Before we experience a real change, if we only want to send people for a seminar, it will not work very well. They will not be captivated by our (daily) family way of life. That is why through the Home Group we are looking for a real change in our lives. First the invited guests must experience that the Home Group can help them in their life, then naturally be won over and study the Divine Principle.

If we are having difficulties within our family, there is no reason to feel shame, because after we have overcome that, we would have the best testimony to help other people.

Development of Assistant Leaders

With activities of the greater Church only, it would take a long time to produce assistant leaders. But if you open small groups (Home Groups), you would be creating the same number of leaders as there are Home Groups. Each time a Home Group multiplies the number of leaders increases. The Home Groups work to create leaders through giving them the opportunity to take care of other members.

Leaders of Home Groups must be mini parents. Through leading the Home Groups, they will have opportunities to develop the heart of parents. Also they will be trained to care for and love Cain. In this way, you can grow the heart of responsibility like Abel.

The Mission of Abel that all Leaders must remember to practice

Abel should love, protect and restore Cain. Through this, it helps the development of Cain. Abel must show an example of the life of faith, of love, of victory, etc. Abel must show a vision. This will facilitate the victory of Cain through love.

If Abel acts on his fallen nature, it will not help Cain gain a victory.

Abel should digest any "persecution" through love and patience (persecution here means any situation that strikes the heart of Abel).

Abel must make the separation of Satan through the Cain and Abel relationship and Cain should be saved through being given responsibilities, receiving guidance, etc.

Abel must restore the birth-right through subjugating Cain naturally, through love and self-sacrifice.

Leaders must be "parents" who have matured in love like Cain and Abel. When he has overcome his fallen nature as Cain and Abel the leader can acquire the heart of parents.

The expression "heart of a parent in the shoes of a servant" means that externally he/she serves as a servant, but with a heart of the father/mother. Within the heart of parents there is no place for judgment.

If the desire to judge Cain arises in Abel's heart, he is still not feeling the parent's heart. He himself has to realise that he needs to improve. (he/she)

Forming new Home Groups

Except for the time of the Sunday Service, we can choose any day of the week to hold Home Group meetings. It is essential to have the meetings once a week and not once every 2 weeks, because if this happens, the development of the Home Group and spiritual growth will be very much prolonged.

The main objective of the Home Group is Tribal Messiahship. This concept is different from the concept of brotherhood, trinities or making witnessing teams.

We can establish our Home Groups with 3 or 4 families together. This will give between 6, 8 or 10 people. It is not good to begin a Home Group with 12 people, because the group would already be full, you would not have enough space for new guests to join.

The process of starting a Home Group should be officially organised through the local church leader (pastor or missionary) whoever is the Central Figure. This avoids problems between the members in the formation of the group. The pastor or missionary is in the position of parents and must be consulted regarding any situation with the Home Group.

To count the number of participants, we must count only those who actively participate during the discussion time about the reading in the Home Group. In the case of children, if they are mature enough to engage in discussion about reading, they can be counted as members of the Home Group.

To prevent children from interrupting the Home Group meeting, you may appoint someone to care for them in another room. You could also create another Home Group for young people to carry out meetings separately.

If by chance the husband and wife participate together in the Home Group, they count as two separate people. Attendance is counted per person and not per family.

Depending on the subject at the Home Group meeting, it is not appropriate for unmarried/young people to participate. For example, with topics about conjugal relationships. In this case, you can place the children in another room for them to have their own meeting, with more appropriate content. Some Home Groups already experienced this and reported that the result was very positive. Both adults and young people liked to meet in this way.

Deciding the Leader.

Each Home Group should choose its own leader and assistant leader. The assistant leader is someone who is preparing to be the leader of the next Home Group when multiplication takes place.

From the beginning of the formation of a Home Group, you have to prepare and train the next leader by working together.

Suggestions: once a month the leader of the Home Group could allow the assistant leader to lead a meeting of the Home Group so that he can develop confidence and skill. The leader would only support it, without evaluating.

What is the single most important thing to be a Leader of Home Group?

The most valuable and important quality (ability) to be a leader is not knowledge, but is to have love! We need not worry too much whether or not we have adequate external skills to lead a Home Group; we only need to invest love in each member and each guest. This is sufficient for the Home Group to develop and multiply. Many regular members, who are not leaders or lecturers, are having success as leaders of Home Groups.

Let's look at the testimony of Mrs. Joise dos Santos. She joined the church in 2008, received the blessing and became the leading member of a Home Group in 2013:

"We had a very challenging beginning because I had no experience of leading groups. I thought that I would not be able to do it because I had no experience as a lecturer or speaking in public. At first we had some difficulties even to set weekly goals, but through the efforts of each person, we became successful. Little by little, as love began to unfold and grow, victories became visible. Today the Home Group "The Origin", has a nice feeling of love and a harmonious and heavenly atmosphere.

When guests join, they feel comfortable and confident to share. The guests even open their hearts by saying that it is very good to participate in the meetings and enjoy the atmosphere. Our Home Group already multiplied from the first level, giving rise to a new Home Group

"Relatives and Friends". Delighted with this victory, we offer our work to God and to True Parents. We are determined to organise our efforts to further improve the activities"!

Joise Nascimento dos Santos (leading "The Origin" Home Group)

Some differences between Home Groups and the Church.

- The Home Group is not supposed to create a parallel to the church. In other words, it is not to increase the number of people and remain as a large, growing church. When the number increases to more than 12 people, you should multiply. (Depending on the situation and in an appropriate manner we can have a little flexibility on this number).
- The greater church (local Church) must be central.
- It is not proper to use names of people for the Home Group, for example "John's Home Group", "Mary's Home Group", etc.
- Home Groups need an identity for example with logos, flags and t-shirts (shirts). Each Home Group can make a website and post photos, testimonies, etc. (links from any site, can be placed on an official national Home Groups website).

Chapter 3.
The Five Essential Elements of a Home Group

The essential elements of a Home Group

The following are the essential elements of a Home Group meeting, although they don't need to be in this order:

1. Worship or Praise (prayer and worship music).

This is the worship element of the Home Group, but does not include a sermon.

2. Fellowship (friendship and union between the members).

Breaks in the Home Group meeting are a good opportunity for this.

3. Study of the Word (reading and discussion about the reading).

The reading should not be long. This reading is intended to guide the subject for the discussion later. The theme of the reading should be easy for people to comment on, because if it is a very sensitive issue, people will feel difficult talking about it. The leader of Home Group should be able to fit the content of the reading on a single sheet and distribute to participants at the time of the reading. This will make it easier when you get to the discussion and also demonstrates the sincere investment of the leader and love for each participant in their Home Group. One suggestion is to email the reading the day before to the group members to study and consider prior to the meeting. In this case be sensitive to new guests who will be reading the content for the first time.

4. Practise ("Weekly Goal" for a real change in the life of the members)

Practise daily and assess every seven days (in the Home Group meetings).

5. Witness (connecting new people. Care, educate and multiply)

If you do not have these elements the Home Group will become only a social gathering, or closed group. A dead group is one where the members never bring new guests and don't strive to grow.

Each of these five elements is important: 1 - Worship, 2 - Fellowship, 3 - Study of the Word, 4 - Practise, 5 – Witnessing

Note:

1. If we only emphasize fellowship in the Home Group, the meeting will be nothing more than a social gathering.
2. If you only have the elements of worship, fellowship and study of the word, the Home Group will become just a closed community that meets between members and does not grow and expand. It would become a kind of study meeting.

3. If you only have worship, study of the word and witnessing, you will be missing the joy of union between friends and the acts or practises that cause real change in our lives.
4. Without actual growth, you will be looking for results only in external activities and you may rapidly become discouraged, both internally and externally.
   You need connection between the external activities and the internal growth of love. The development of external activities must go along with the growth of love, just like two gears, which rotate together and should not be disconnected.
5. If the Home Group has all the elements, except the element of practise through the "Weekly Goal", you will be in a situation where you won't have any connection between testimonies and what you have learnt in the Home Group. If you don't practise, there won't be any real change occurring in your lives. If the Group Leader lacks inspiration and growth, they are unable to inspire and give testimonies based on their own experience; it prevents learning in the Home Group and prevents development of its members. This also has the potential to discouraging any guests.
6. If we only witness and ignore the other essential elements, it would become a model similar to a mobilisation of teams for outside activities. Our witnessing should be through "Oikos (Home Church)", which means to bear witness to the people through our daily experience. In the chapter on Oikos (Home Church) we'll address this issue more extensively.

Example of a Home Group meeting schedule

1. Greetings and Prayer

Sometimes when the Home Group consists of members only, you can bow to True Parents before you begin, but if you have guests, you must act appropriately to avoid unease or misunderstanding. In this case, you can skip this part. The prayer does not need to be long; guests might not have the patience or understanding to wait through a long prayer.

2. Songs

The Home Group does not only have to sing FFWPU songs. You can sing other praise and worship songs as well. This will make it easier for guests to join in to the Home Group.

3. Reading and Discussion about the reading

When we are with Christians, we can prepare an additional Bible verse that is related to the content of the reading.

The reading should not be long. The purpose of the reading should be for reflection on life, to discover the "weekly goal" and then to practise what you learn. It would be good if each person brings a notebook to jot down what touched their heart.

In the same way that the pastor makes personal conditions when preparing the sermon, select some paragraphs from the books of True Parents, for example: Cheon Seong Gyeong, with the right content to guide the later discussion. This in itself is good training for the leader of the Home Group. At the Home Group meeting, you can hand out a sheet with the reading to all the participants. It can be read one or two times to facilitate the discussion about the content. If you are unable to prepare a worksheet, you can read directly from the book.

Following the reading, we must talk about the subject which was read. It is important that **all the members strive to talk**, since this will contribute positively to the atmosphere of the meeting. If our members do not speak, the guests will not feel free to speak.

No one should attempt to change or correct anyone.

Now and then, after someone (member or guest) makes a comment, without realising it, we try to fix and change it. This shouldn't be done in the Home Group meeting, as it makes people feel uncomfortable. When we correct or fix something that a member or guest said during the meeting, they may not return for future meetings, because they will feel that they were not accepted. We don't need to worry if their views are initially a little out of line with The Principle. Normally when they receive the One-to-one tuition, they will learn more deeply about The Principle and will change their point of view. There was a case in which a Home Group guest's opinion was out of line with The Principle but no one tried to fix it or correct it at the time. After a period of time participating in a Home Group and receiving One-to-one tuition, he received the Blessing. When a new guest joins the Home Group they are a new-born baby, they only need love, acceptance and care to grow and develop.

The one hour of discussion and reading, is not a time to discuss the matter and reach a common conclusion. Also it is not for each person repeat the content that was read. The leader must allow each person to express **his or her views freely** on the subject. The guest can also speak on the point that **touched their heart or** something that caught their attention.

During Home Group meetings we must train ourselves to:

Speak Appropriately:

In the Home Group we must speak in a positive manner, <u>without the multiplication of evil</u> (for example: criticism, pride, arrogance, resentment etc.) Even if the subject matter is negative, it is possible to discuss it without multiplication of evil. We need to know that **<u>"speaking appropriately is a way of loving".</u>**

How can we check if the way of speaking is negative or positive?

We can check if the way we talk is positive or negative based on the Divine Principle. See the 4 main categories of fallen nature at "The Difference between Sin and Fallen Nature (The Way to Eliminate Fallen Nature)" on page 41.

In summary the 4 Categories of Fallen Nature:

1. Not taking God's point of view
2. Leaving your own position.
3. Reversal of dominion.
4. Multiplication of evil

We must take care not to confuse "freedom of opinion" with "freedom to not take God's point of view".

Within the Home Group we can train ourselves to speak without displaying fallen nature.

We can talk about difficult situations, but we should not speak with a negative attitude and position. If we do not overcome this point, the Home Group will break down as it will be losing the essence needed to give a good result.

Listen Well:

During the Home Group, we must listen to the other people with interest, even if we do not agree 100% with their arguments so the people will feel loved and valued. We must not correct or interrupt the opinion of people during a Home Group meeting. If we do so, people will feel judged and will be discouraged. Often people are not only looking for answers, but also want to open their hearts. If that is the case and we take time to listen, it will ease their hearts. The member who is witnessing and brings a guest also needs to know that we are listening well to their guests. We need to know that **"Good Listening is a way of loving"**

We must avoid our Home Group appearing to be or becoming a place of "evaluation". An evaluation leader is a person or member that is only waiting for someone to talk to gauge their opinion and is always correcting, arranging or trying to explain what they are saying in a different way. When there is a person like this in the Home Group, people do not want to speak freely, since they will have fear of being evaluated by that person. The members of the Home Group should not train to be an "evaluator". The Home Group works very well when all accept all with an open heart, without evaluating the opinion of the other. People may speak freely because they feel accepted by all, loved, respected and valued. In the Home Group love must always be greater than the conflict between the different views.

4. Establishment and Evaluation of the "Weekly Goal"

The "Weekly Goal" must be something that has a direct connection with attaining "individual perfection" (elimination of fallen nature and the growth of love).

The "Weekly Goal" is the component that will drive the Home Group, because it leads to real change in our lives, eliminating fallen natures and growing true love. This is the essence of the Home Group, and other parts such as reading, prayer and discussion are there to support the success of the "Weekly Goal".

To establish the "Weekly Goal" we should follow these steps:

1. Each person discovers, within themselves, something that disturbs or hinders their relationships with others.
2. Then, they create concrete goals which guide their conscious struggle to overcome something in their day to day lives,;
3. They should also pray and offer conditions to receive spiritual strength helping them to overcome the test;
4. At each Home Group meeting, assess progress and make a new determination based on the Weekly Goal.

5. Seeing change in other members of the Home Group will motivate the rest of the group.
6. It is not obligatory to talk publicly about individual goals or evaluate the past week if people don't want to or it's not appropriate.
7. It is important that everyone is prepared to struggle to sincerely engage with the "Weekly Goal", because the essence the Home Group is that each participant **changes himself through** fighting and defeating their weaknesses, by choosing a "Weekly Goal" to ensure the growth of love.

Examples of some appropriate Weekly Goals:

1. Until the next Home Group meeting, I am not going to fight with my wife (or husband) avoiding discussions on specific topics which we know will aggravate each other. (Sometimes we manage to keep calm on several issues, but on others we lose patience quickly and fight. This must be our weak point that we can set as the "Weekly Goal").
2. Until the next Home Group meeting, I'm going to love my wife (or husband) doing something substantial (example: wash the dishes, give a massage, cleaning, etc.) once a day. (In this case there are safeguards, an internal goal and an external goal, so that the internal goal did not become vague or empty. It is important to create a goal that can be practiced).
3. Until the next Home Group meeting, I am going to praise my spouse at least twice a day, discovering the aspects about them that God loves.
4. Until the next Home Group meeting, I am not going to criticise my wife (or husband).
5. Until the next Home Group meeting, I am not going to speak to my children with anger or irritation (i.e. mixed with fallen nature).
6. Until the next Home Group meeting, I would like to be grateful for all the opportunities that arise out of difficult situations, in the context of an intimate relationship, giving me the opportunity to exceed my emotional limitations.

These are some examples of the "Weekly goal" that some people have used and have worked very well.

Examples of inadequate "Weekly goals"

1. I will not fight. (Not specific with whom. It is best to make the "Weekly Goal" a little more real).
2. I'm going to unite as a couple.
3. I'm going to remove my fallen nature.
4. I'll be improving family.
5. I'm going to grow spiritually. (These first 5 items are not specific targets; this makes the practice and measuring success difficult).
6. I'm going to make world peace. (This is outside of reality. Impossible to do in a week).
7. I'm going to serve my wife every day doing domestic work. (Has great potential. It also is not very specific and is difficult to actually practice).
8. I'm not going to bite my nails.

9. I'm not going to drink soft drinks. (These last two goals are not directly connected with the matter of perfection and the individual growth of love).
10. I'm going to do 120 bows.
11. I am going to distribute 12 autobiographies in the next week. (These items can be targets of external activities. But it is not appropriate for the "Weekly Goal" in the Home Group, because it is not directly linked with the matter of the individual perfection and growth of love).
12. I'm not going to be intolerant. (This goal will produce an effect contrary to the purpose of the "Weekly Goal").

    One way to discover the "Weekly Goal" is to have a candid discussion within the individual families, in which each one can speak frankly about how the others could improve. But this must be done in an appropriate environment and not transformed into argument and accusation.

Method for establishing a "Weekly Goal"

Through reading Cheon Song Gyeong and the discussion, God can inspire each person about their "Weekly Goal".

Especially during the discussion in the Home Group, God can use some issue or someone's comment to touch their hearts.

When someone in the Home Group makes a comment about something and you feel that God is giving a message to you at that moment, this is an opportunity to establish your "Weekly Goal"

A person can ask their husband, wife, or children. They will always have a heartfelt response, for example, "Daddy, please be like this and not that", "It would be good if you were acting this way and not like that with our children", etc. Sometimes we overlook these types of requests for a long time without noticing.

If a bride and bridegroom establish the "Weekly Goal" together, joining to help each other, it becomes more effective. For this reason, it would be better for the bridegroom and the bride to participate together in the Home Group meeting.

In the Home Group meeting, we pray, read and have discussions. This allows time for reflection on our life. After this, we can establish our "Weekly Goal" and practice it daily until the next meeting.

At the next meeting each person does a self-assessment on whether they fulfilled the goal and then resets the goal with a higher standard (if already fulfilled, you can increase the standard or in the case of not having fulfilled, re-establish the same goal). It is not a requirement to speak publicly about the subject of the goal if a person doesn't want, but it is necessary to establish it, otherwise growth will not happen.

It would be a good idea for each person to have an "Individual Improvement" journal to aid memory, practice and motivation to overcome. After a period of time you will have a lot of important content saved in that notebook.

Whenever we create a "Weekly Goal", the difficulties in that area of life will increase, but we must not lose patience or become discouraged, as it is bound to happen like that. Simply, we must pray and do conditions to remove our fallen nature. Each week that we are successful, the power of the fallen nature will decline and our spiritual strength will increase. The top is very difficult, but little by little it becomes easier and if we persist in the goal, we'll be able to completely eradicate that type of problem and we will feel free. Some members had good experiences that when they established the "Weekly Goal" and achieved it, they were able to solve difficulties that had been in the family for a long time and real changes happened in their lives.

5. Prayer

If any member or guest requests a prayer for any purpose; at that time we all can pray for that purpose.

6. Notices

If you have any notices, for example: the introduction of someone who is coming for the first time or if there are any events to report about or to announce, memorial days, Holy Days, meetings, etc… this would be the ideal time and helps the Home Group be connected with the greater Church.

7. Summary of the Meeting by the Leader of the Home Group

The leader of the Home Group makes a small summary of the important points of the meeting. Also you must resolve any misunderstanding that might have occurred on the part of any guest (for example, a member said something which the guest understands differently; if the leader of the Home Group perceived the situation, you can repeat what the member wanted to say so the guest will be able to understand). Whilst doing this you should avoid evaluation or expressing the opinion overly strongly.

8. Coffee Break/informal discussion

Sometimes members and guests want to talk about other topics. This is the time to talk more openly about other matters and not only the subject of the reading.

How to choose the topics for the Home Group meeting

When the leader of the Home Group prepares the theme for the reading, he needs to think about preparing readings that help:

1 growth of love in a person's daily life,

2 individual development,

3 the connection between couples, and

4 how to complete the formula course.

This is the official direction for the work of the Home Groups in Brazil. To set "weekly goals" you must also follow the same direction.

Examples of suitable topics for reading and discussion

To prepare topics for the Home Group meeting, we must focus on issues such as the unity of a couple (identifying problems and ways to overcome conflict), the education of children (relationships between parents and children), the 4 types of heart in the family (children, siblings, couples and parents), the ideal family, the existence of life after death, the value of life (the purpose of life), relationships at work, in school, with neighbours and friends, real friendship and others.

Examples of inappropriate topics for discussion in the Home Group

1. What is the meaning of the Providential Declaration of the Messiah by True Parents of Heaven, Earth and Humanity in the year 2010? (This item is very difficult to understand and does not touch the topic directly related the growth of love).
2. What is the best brand of HD (hard drive) to save images on a computer? (This subject is far too limited. It has no connection with the matter of the growth of my love and practice of how to complete the formula course).
3. What will happen with a particular character in the next chapter of this novel? (This subject is too secular).
4. What is the exact definition of the "Industrial Revolution" according to the Divine Principle? (This matter is too academic).

Also if the meeting consists only of members, we should avoid topics/readings that do not have a direct connection with the goal of "individual perfection" and "marriage", (= growth of love) and the realization of the three great blessings.

We must also avoid issues such as football, politics, social issues, economics, films, programs on television or talk about any specific religion (these subjects can distract from the main focus of the Home Group).

Depending on the situation, in the fellowship section or during the break in the meeting you can touch on these issues, but should avoid discussions on them during the meeting itself and during the establishment and evaluation of the "Weekly Goal", because it will distract from this purpose. We must avoid negative reactions, resentment, criticism, accusations, doubt (questioning) on the providential address that was given to us. The secret of the success of the Home Group is to not speak negatively (multiplication of evil). We need only multiply goodness; if you multiply evil, the Home Group will become a "cancer cell". We must avoid getting into a situation where our Home Group becomes a meeting to gossip.

It is possible to talk about a difficult situation without multiplying evil (that doesn't mean that you should hide a difficult situation and report only positive things to the central figure). Even when you are talking about a difficult situation, the way of speaking determines whether you are multiplying evil or not. It is possible to pass all the information you want to pass, without multiplying any evil. When we talk about blaming others, we are talking about ways to multiply evil (for example, he is bad, he is terrible, he does not have love, for that reason I have the same problem ...). But if we are talking about taking responsibility ourselves, this will be the positive way to talk about: (for example, if I love more, if I can overcome, I understand that I must, forgive, etc...).

Role of the Home Group leader

Clearly the leader has the mission to educate and teach; but the main concept of leadership that we want to cultivate in Home Groups is that the leader must serve in order to give direction – with the heart of a father (parent) in the shoes of a servant. The only thing that we need in order to be the leader of a Home Group is **love**. If we have love, or the willingness to develop our love, we can be the leader of a Home Group.

The main mission of the Leader of a Home Group is to "listen more and talk less"

In the discussion about the reading, the Home Group leader should not give a sermon and must not speak for a long time, giving directions, teaching or giving all the answers. If only the leader speaks, you will stray from the original aim of the small group, which is to give satisfaction to each of its members. The leader must take the role of MC (master of ceremonies) or facilitator who encourages others to open their hearts and speak. The Home Group leader must train to listen to others well by applying the principle of 8:2 or 9:1 - Listen 8 and talk 2 or listen 9and talk 1. The leader should not give a sermon or internal guidance which dominates the entire Home Group. There are situations however where the leader needs to talk a little more to help open the hearts of the rest of the group.

Difficulties faced by Home Group leaders

Sometimes members do not want to be Home Group leaders because they think that a Home Group leader has to teach, offer solutions, or give sermons. But in truth the leader of a Home Group has no such function so there is no need to worry about that.

Teaching vs. Coaching

"Coaching" gives more autonomy, a two way dialog helping a person to discover the answer for himself. "Teaching" controls more, creating a one way dialog which shows the way directly.

Our leadership style in the Home Group is closer to that of a "coach" than a "teacher". A football coach accompanies the group personally, working together until they achieve a real change. The Home Group leader must do the same thing, accompanying the growth and development of each of its members.

The spirit of "coaching" in the Home Group

Everyone in the world has infinite potential as the individual incarnation of God. Any answer that a person needs exists within themselves. In the Home Group, we should encourage people to find the answers only from within their original mind. That is why anyone can be a leader of a Home Group. Beyond transmitting knowledge, they must also focus on real transformation in the lives of the members. Pastors and missionaries are professionals and outside the Home Group meeting they can give specific direction, teach and give answers directly, but the leader of the Home Group does not need to extend to that level, you need only encourage people to find the answers in their original minds.

A technique of "coaching" in the Home Group

You must first listen well with care and concern. Next you must then ask appropriate questions. After receiving answers, you must then feed-back and allow the person to discover the answer for themselves. This is the mission of the leader of the Home Group. Up to that level, the leader of the Home Group completes their mission. When we listen to someone with love, attention and respect, we are giving relief to the heart of this person.

Listen Attentively

There are different levels of listening. Through our attitude we can check which level we are at. There is either an egocentric way or a way that focuses on the other person. We must train ourselves to listen to other people and focus on them.

The egocentric way (focusing on yourself): Ignoring what they are really saying, pretending that you are listening. This will not ease the heart of the other person. Another case is when the person is listening, but filtering the content: accepts some of the content and rejects or condemns other parts, or gets nervous, disinterested and even negative.

Focusing on others: listening well and actively. Seeking to understand the thoughts and intent of the person who is speaking. Without judging whether the content is right or wrong, we must accept the person speaking entirely. Listening well does not mean that we are agreeing with some wrong content that the person might be saying; however through love, we are accepting the person speaking. When our own children say something wrong, this does not diminish our relationship with them. We need to hear the other person's feelings. We must make an investment of heart. In addition we need to feel the heart of the person that we are listening to and we will grow to a level of heart to release the hearts of others, by simply listening.

When we are trying to ease the heart of a person through a discussion, we must first listen more and then talk less. But, more important than listening is entirely accepting the person as a child of God and we must share his feelings empathetically. It will be easier to share their feelings and console them if we have already personally had similar experiences (for example, a person who has gone through an illness or disease would find it easier to comfort a person going through a similar situation). If we have achieved victory in a similar situation to that which the other person is facing, we will have increased the level of our understanding and that is why we will further alleviate their heart (for example: if we have already experienced, through love, many difficult situations between Cain and Abel. As a result it will be easier to understand the heart of a person who is facing the same situation of conflicts that we already had some success in). Because of our victory, we increase the level of love and we acquire a higher level of heart that can give relief others.

In the Home Group, listening is a form of training to love just as talking is also training to love. We self-train to talk and listen without expressing our fallen nature.

Ask questions

After listening well, we must ask questions properly to help the person discover the answer within their original mind. There are some questions which are not appropriate or adequate.

Examples of inadequate questions (includes closed questions requiring a simple one word answer): "Why did you do that?" "Did you do it?", "What have you been doing until now?", "Did you do it correctly?", "Why didn't you do it correctly?". These questions look like a heavy interrogation looking for the cause and reason. These types of questions ask for precise answers (they cause pressure, do not relieve the heart and do not help the person find the answer in their original mind).

Examples of appropriate questions (open questions): "In this case, what do you think it would be better to do? ", "What did you think, what is your opinion? ", "What can we do to improve things? ", "Where could we begin?". These types of questions allow several options for responses and do not put pressure on a person to search for accurate answers. The person then, can reflect and find the answers that are already in their original mind.

If the leader or some other person within the Home Group begins to dominate the meeting by giving "sermons" and strong explanations (even though logically correct), the other members will close their hearts and will not feel comfortable to express themselves. They will not speak and won't open their hearts, since they will fear being corrected by that person.

Feedback

To be in a position to give good feedback (listening, supporting, encouraging, praising or giving your suggestions and opinion) to a person, you have to observe the principle of 8:2 (listen 8 and talk 2). We must do this in a positive way, being real and sincere. We must always encourage improvement by providing support for real change in the life of the person. Finally, we must always encourage, support and praise everyone within the Home Group.

When a person is facing some difficulty or barrier, we must support them and encourage them to find the motivation to overcome. When he succeeds, we must give praise and share in their happiness.

Summary - The Focus of the Home Group

We should listen well, use the right questions, give good feedback, responding with praise and encouragement (support) and using the 8:2 principle, where the leader of the Home Group speaks less and guides members to talk more.

We must not: dominate the entire discussion; interrupt the comments of another; discuss; express emotions and uncontrolled explosive reactions; draw attention to ourselves; give orders; try to educate others; change the subject selfishly and not give opportunities to other people to express their ideas; make sermons or give internal guidance lectures; or, finally, remain silent by saying that there is nothing to talk about (we have to strive to speak and thus contribute to the good atmosphere of the Home Group meeting).

When we multiply the Home Groups often, it is likely that each blessed family will become the leader of a Home Group and progress further in the multiplication process, it is also possible that the new members will become Home Group leaders. For the Home Group to work in this situation, the mission/role of the Home Group leader is established at a basic level, it is relatively simple to do, such that everyone could lead a Home Group. The leader of Home Group does not require great skill, only needs to have love.

How Home Groups differ from Sunday Service and the Rules of the Home Group

The leader of Home Group does not teach, but only helps people to find the answers in their own conscience.

The obstacle that prevents God giving us his love and doing his work is not in the Church system, the Sunday Service system, the Home Group system, the Cain and Abel system, etc..., but it is the fallen nature within each of us. It is not any system that prevents the flow of God's love. Both the style of the sermon, as well as the styles of Home Groups, if we do not manifest fallen natures, God feels free to manifest in our environment.

Unlike a Sunday sermon, where the Pastor "must speak" and we are able experience that God speaks through an official as the central figure and representative of God; in the Home Group the leader "must not talk too much", since through the Home Group system we can experience the work of God freely through the action of giving and receiving between the participants. The Home Group leader does not need to worry about teaching people; but only help them to find the answer in their own conscience.

We can experience that when a person is speaking his opinion freely, without trying to change or correct anyone, the other people present feel that God is using the other person to send them a message and improve their lives. Many times, after hearing someone's comment, we begin to think of any changes that we have to make in our lives. This is the work of God within the Home Group. But if we start trying to change or correct others intentionally, that will cause a blocking of this wonderful work of God.

Rules of the Home Groups

Rule 1: you should not give sermons.

The leader must avoid giving long sermons and heavy guidance, because this can block the work of God. The role of the leader, in the Home Group meeting, is closer to a MC (master of ceremonies) or facilitator than that of a speaker. Then the leader should not give a sermon nor internal guidance during the Home Group meeting. The leader will not talk much, but this does not mean that the Home Group loses its opinion leader. He continues with his position and function as a centre for the Home Group meetings and activities.

Rule 2: We must empty our minds to make space for God.

Through his Sunday sermon, we have experienced that God works through the preacher, but in the Home Group we have to create a situation so that we can feel that God is working within the action of giving and receiving between members, playing the original mind of each one. The leader must empty his mind and maintain an attitude of mediator and not be overbearing. If the leader has his mind full of his own ideas, that will ultimately cause the rejection of the ideas and opinions of others.

Rule 3: Nobody should try to change another person.

Do not try to change one another. In the Home Group we don't have to worry about trying to give words to change other people. We should be concerned about how to change ourselves first. This will allow you to experience that your personal change caused a transformation in the other people. We know that it is not easy to change ourselves, then in the same way, it is difficult to change other people. The Home Group will work correctly only if each person attempts to change only himself. In that case, God will be free to move to everyone.

Rule 4: Do not lose your patience concluding the discussion quickly. Allow each person to discover the answer for himself.

The Home Group leader must have patience to avoid correcting the other, and not giving direction, immediate responses or strong and direct education. It is important that the leader directs each person to be the one who discovers the answers for themselves through the discussion in the Home Group. The leader must encourage each one to speak freely in accordance with his original mind. Sometimes it may happen that the leader already knows the answer or he already knows how to respond in a particular case, but he must not give the answer directly (example: "in that case you must do the same as I did, to improve on this or change such an attitude" or "The way to resolve must be like this"... etc.) If he does that the leader will be preventing the person from discovering the answer within his original mind for himself. The leader should not finish quickly but has to give the appropriate time for everyone, through discussion, to arrive at their answers in due course. If not resolved during a meeting he must maintain patience and know what the process to resolve the issue is. When that person finds the answer, without forcing it, it will remain within him for ever.

The Reason that we must not give a "Sermon" or "Internal Guidance" in the weekly Home Group meeting.

The five essential elements of the Home Group are:

1. Worship (prayer, holy songs)
2. Fellowship (friendship, snacks, tea)
3. Study of the Word (IIDII style followed by discussion about reading)
4. Practice (Weekly Goal leading to real change in family life and support to complete the Formula Course)
5. Witnessing (through the involvement of new people, love, serve, care for and educate. One-to-one Seminar until the multiplication of the Home Group)

1. The First Reason

If we give sermons and internal guidance during the Home Group meeting, although the contents may be good and helpful in the life of the members, the meeting will remain simply at the level of "regular meetings between members for the study of the Word", with additional elements of "worship", "fellowship" and "study of the Word". The important elements of "Testimony", "taking care of the guests in the Home Group environment" and the "national explosion of witnessing" will all be missing and growth is unlikely to take place.

2. Second Reason

In addition, members are going to feel that the Home Group is merely "a meeting for a small sermon", outside the usual hours of the Sunday Service. They won't reach the previous level of excitement. When we give a sermon or internal guidance in the weekly Home Group meeting, we will face the difficulty of adapting the content to satisfy the old and new guests at the same time. For this reason, it will be difficult to look after new guests and it will become a closed Home Group that obstructs the inflow of new people.

3. Third reason

Practice through the "Weekly Goal". This part works to connect all the other parts of the meeting. When the spiritual parent performs acts of love through the "Weekly Goal" he will be better trained to love and win over his spiritual children.

4. Fourth Reason

A sermon in the Home Group can cut off the flow of the process of witnessing that is:

1. through the Word, as we engage in discussion about the reading.
2. by means of the discussion about the reading, we can determine the "Weekly Goal".
3. through the fulfilment of the "Weekly Goal", each person grows and improves their relationships with others including their marriage relationship.
4. By experiencing the growth of love, each person can take care of their guests.

5. Fifth Reason

Delivering sermons and internal guidance decreases the time to share deeply and share the personal situation of each participant during the discussion about the reading. When the Home Group leader expresses his opinion strongly, taking advantage of his position, the participants will avoid saying something which is not in agreement with the leader's view and the discussion about the reading will not be very effective in opening the hearts of the participants.

6. Sixth Reason

The main focus of the weekly Home Group meeting is to open the heart of the invited guest and witness to them, through the establishment of a culture of dialog focussed on the reading. If you don't establish a situation during the discussion where anyone can give their opinion freely, acceptance by the guests will be limited. Although some guests may express an opinion that is not in accordance with the Principle, we must not lose patience and try to correct it immediately. Later, when they receive the One-to-one Seminar, *that* will be the opportunity to educate them more deeply.

We explained that we must not give sermons or internal guidance but depending on the situation, a short explanation may be necessary. For example, in the case where guests are beginners and do not understand what you mean when reading the Cheon Seong Gyeong.

In that case, the leader can provide a short explanation after the reading and only after you started the discussion about the reading based on that topic.

Also, at the end of the discussion, it would be good if the Home Group leader spoke briefly summarizing the contents of the discussions, giving emphasis to some important points. The Home Group leader must avoid talking and dominating the entire discussion time. But, on the other hand, when the participants don't want to share their views voluntarily and it is hard to continue, the leader can speak of his life and personal experiences. You can then open the hearts of the participants for them to speak naturally.

Different levels of consultation

The Home Group has limitations in caring for (resolving) the situations of the guests or members with individual and marital problems. There are circumstances in which, depending on the severity, the leader of Home Group must defer to the local pastor, who will take care of the situation. Also, be aware that there are cases that only the Blessed Families Department can solve.

Ice breakers

Especially at the beginning of a new group, there are times when the atmosphere of the Home Group meeting can seem a bit downhearted. In these situations, people will need help to open their hearts and express themselves. The Home Group leader can use some of the ice breaker questions at the end of this manual. The ice breakers will help people relax and open their hearts, thus improving the atmosphere of the meeting. From there, we can run the meeting with more confidence. You can also use some kind of dynamic game to open the hearts of individuals and relax them all (examples: hot potato, repeat the name of the fruit, Riddles, etc...) You might have some kind of joke of appropriate uplifting content. It is also good that the leader or any member of the Home Group talk about their personal experience. This will help to break down the barriers for the participants.

Additional Home Group meeting for taking care of guests

Once you begin to develop the Home Group, you will probably need to have an additional meeting, only between the members, to deal with any issues that are not suitable to discuss in front of the guests. For example, have a prayer meeting to ensure that guests can become members, a meeting to decide who is going to do One-to-one Seminars with the guests, and to share the real situation of each guest and make prayer conditions for them.

Prayer Card for the Home Group

In the Home Group where they're all saying prayers for each other, the room is transformed in a loving and heavenly environment. Prayer does not need to be very long. There was a case in which the members of the Home Group made prayer of 4 minutes for each other, every day, and immediately experienced a great unity of heart and a different atmosphere. A suggestion is to prepare a prayer card for the Home Group.

Write the name of the Home Group and of each of the members. Making a prayer for yourselves will accelerate the process for the Home Group to become a "loving nest".

On the reverse, put the name of each guest and the spiritual parents. All members then make a daily prayer, once a day for members and guests. All the Home Group members take care of their guests and make mutually supportive prayers. One Group reported that they are running a witnessing event because they have been thinking and praying for their Home Group 24 hours per day. Making prayers for the Home Group members will increase the ratio of heart among the members. Where there is love, multiplication will occur.

The Home Group is a system where all take care of the guests, as a family

When we don't have Home Groups, each spiritual parent cares only for his own spiritual child, but, after the Home Groups, all the members together nurture and give love to your guests.

The Home Group is not only a weekly meeting. The Home Group is an experience of the Kingdom of Heaven. Communication between the Home Group members should continue during the week, for example, phone calls, sending messages, visiting, mutually living for one another.

Larger Group and Small Group (Greater Church and Small Church)

The larger group and the smaller group develop together in perfect harmony. This is the model of a healthy church. The relationship between the two is like two wings of a bird. It requires a good balance between the two for the bird to be able to fly.

Everything for the development of the Home Groups, from leader training to the processes (Home Group Introduction events, multiplication, etc.), should be completely centralized through the local leader (pastor or missionary). The members of the Home Group must participate in the Sunday Service without fail. The Home Group should not replace the Sunday Service and the Sunday Service should not replace the Home Group.

The greater church should allow the maximum creativity of all the Home Groups (hobbies, sport, music, cultural activities, etc.).

The mission of the Greater Church (Large Group)

1. Caring

The leader of the greater church (city headquarters or regional official mission) should have the role of traveling, visiting, caring and loving each Home Group; conducting seminars regularly with the Home Group leaders (and assistant leaders) receiving reports and experiences; help the Home Group leaders with their difficulties in managing and guiding their Home Groups. He should always be prepared to receive them and discuss with them. The leader of the greater church must do a great deal in this mission, visiting Home Groups many times because it may happen that some months later the Home Groups can get discouraged.

2. Programming

The greater church should provide for the meetings, ideas, materials, words, events and schedules. We must always make the Home Group meeting purposeful, lively and interesting.

3. Events

The church prepares regular events for members and guests of the Home Groups to encourage everyone and participate together. The Home Groups can support when it is necessary to make some mass mobilization; as for example, some providential event.

You can present a sermon for the Home Group guests once a month. For example, on the 1st, 2nd and 3rd Sunday of the month, give sermon for members with high level content and on the 4th Sunday present a sermon for the Home Group guests, preparing content appropriate for them, with shorter duration and also preparing some fellowship after the service.

Every pastor and every mission State every 2 or 3 months should organise a state or regional Home Groups event preparing flags and T-shirts of each Home Group.

Important elements for successful Home Groups

As we emphasized at the start, it is very important that we clearly understand the essence and purpose of the Home Group for its proper growth. Below, we highlight some points that have already been dealt with in the text. This is to facilitate our understanding and practice of Home Group activities.

1. Songs and prayer

Prayer need not be long. There is no requirement to sing only Holy Songs. You may also use other songs from other song books. This will be easier for the witnessing guests. We must not use songs with fallen lyrics however.

2. Ice Breakers

Consider some short game to relax and open the hearts of the participants. The leader can organise an ice breaker if he feels it is necessary.

3. Short Reading

The reading should not be long. Its content has to allow people to comment on later. The Home Group leader should search for the text a day before through prayer and inspiration from God. Print the contents on a single sheet and distribute to the participants at the time of reading or read directly from the book (Cheon Seong Gyeong and World Scripture 2 are recommended).

4. Discussion about the reading

This time is to talk about **and listen properly to each other about** the subject, which was just read. It is important that all members make an effort to share something, because that will contribute positively to the atmosphere of the meeting **"No one attempts to change or correct the other"** – it is not a time to discuss the matter and reach a conclusion, also it is not for each person explain logically their understanding of the content that was read. Each person speaks **his opinion** freely on the subject, or something that has **touched their heart** or something that caught their attention.

In the Home Group we must train ourselves to:

SPEAK APPROPRIATELY: we must speak in a positive manner and without multiplying evil (for example: criticism, pride, arrogance, resentment, etc. are ways of talking by multiplying evil) even if the subject matter was poor, it can always be addressed without multiplying evil. **"Speaking appropriately is one way of loving"**

LISTEN WELL: we must listen with attention and interest to people who do not agree 100% with your argument. Why? People will feel loved and valued. We must not correct them at the Home Group meeting. If we do so, they will feel judged and will be discouraged. Often people are not looking for direct answers, but only want to open their hearts and in that moment, all we need to do is listen attentively, this will put them at ease. Also during any testimony, listen well because we need to know about our guests. We need to know that **"Listening well is a way to love".**

5. Weekly Goal

This is the main point that will enable the Home Group develop because it causes a real change in our lives, eliminating our fallen nature and increasing our capacity for true love. We must establish our "Weekly Goals" focussed on "growing my love in everyday life" or "my individual perfection", "unity of the couple" and "completing the formula course".

How to make a Home Group event

When we use an external method, perhaps a mass mobilization for some event, for example holding a barbecue; if we do not have a system to "take care" of the guests during and after the event then our effort can be wasted there may be no fruit from our investment.

Using the leaflet distribution method, the percentage of people who respond is very low. Based on past experience, we know that the best is close to 3% response. But the problem is the minimum, which is 0%. If we do not make an investment of heart and love, the result can very easily be zero. Also, we might make a calculation in our minds and begin to think that the mobilization of people depends on the number of leaflets that we can print, so printing 1000 leaflets, 30 people will come, then, if we would like 60 people to respond, we will need to print 2000 leaflets and so on. There will probably come a time when we discover we are wasting money printing leaflets and feel that witnessing is too difficult.

When we do Home Group events, it can be a waste to mobilize people en masse through the distribution of leaflets, only. It is better we invest in those people who are already in some way connected with the Home Groups. So instead, the people we invite to participate in the Home Groups are relatives, friends of the guests of Home Groups, and the people of Oikos (Home Church). In this case, a greater number of people will remain after the event to continue as witnessing contacts.

When the members in Brazil held the first Home Group event in Sao Paulo, it was attended by 350 people. Among these, 30 were guests of the new Home Groups, One-to-one Seminars and Oikos (Home Church). In the second event, 1000 people participated, 88 came for the first time. In the third event, of 2300 participants, 706 (30 %) were invited through the Home Groups. There was a significant increase in the number of guests in the later events and those people who had been invited continued to receive care in the Home Groups and through One-to-one Seminars. In the fourth national Home Group event, connecting the whole of Brazil via the internet, we achieved the participation of 3480 persons, within these 870 (25 %) were invited from new Home Groups, One-to-one and Oikos (Home Church).

After the events, we received positive reports about the experiences of the members and guests. Here is the testimony of Ms. Edilândia Oliveira de Morais, a Home Group leader in Pernambuco, about the 4th national Home Group event:

"This event brought more motivation to people to continue improving their unity of heart. There has been a real change for those participating in the Home Group activities. Mainly in the quality of relationships between the brothers and sisters, marriage partners, parents and children. People have been committed to the weekly goal and have achieved a beautiful harmony in the group. We are cleaning our hearts. The Home Group is really a providence of Heaven."

Through the Home Group events we can work in a way that leaves part of the content to be given later. The Home Group works as a small church that can provide assistance to guests before and after the events, thus enabling a higher witnessing result.

In the Home Group event we see the unique character traits of each Home Group through for example, T-shirts, flags, the presentations and performances from the individual Home Groups, etc. All this increases the unity of heart in the Home Groups.

It is important that the Home Group event has testimonies from invited members and new members, because that will liven up the event and the activities. We can also prepare a song, for example Saranghe, and we can sing together at the end of the event. All the participants are thrilled at that time and we feel a heavenly atmosphere.

The best way to mobilize people for the Home Group events is by daily increasing the number of guests embraced by our Home Groups and taking good care of them.

It would be wonderful if at some point True Mother came to our Nation and we could receive her with a great national Home Group event, mobilizing the whole of our Nation. Surely, she would be very happy, especially when she knew that a large percentage of the participants had been witnessed to only recently.

DNA of the cell of Home Group

The essential quality needed to be a Home Group leader of is not skill or knowledge but to have love.

All organizations face a dilemma: if they increase in number, they may decrease in quality and if they want to maintain the quality it is difficult to increase the numbers.

In the Home Group, we have the concept of the "DNA of the Home Group cell" and this resolves this dilemma perfectly. Because of the DNA of the cell; although the Home Group multiplies and develops, the quality is retained through keeping the essence of the DNA. The essence of the Home Group cell is the correct tradition (victory of love, unity, fulfilling the weekly goal, foundation of faith and substance) that we establish from the first cell. If you multiply the Home Group without establishing that essence, you may lose the quality and lose the essence.

To make a national witnessing explosion, we have to be certain to properly establish the essence in the first cell and multiply it by maintaining that DNA. What is the DNA of the Home Group cell? It is True Parents of Heaven, Earth and Humanity, their words, love and tradition. The tradition of tears, true love, the heart of parents in the shoes of a servant. This is one tradition of the early church. We must inherit the heart and the love of True Parents and that is our essential DNA.

We cannot implement multiplication only externally, we must also achieve internal victory. There are cases in which the Home Groups are multiplying well, that happens when you have the correct DNA.

Multiplication

We must begin each Home Group with the intention of multiplying within a certain period of time. We must form the Home Groups with the motivation to win many spiritual children and with the joy of multiplication. Each time we form a new Home Group cell we must establish a goal, for example, we will carry out the first multiplication within 6 months. All Home Groups must do activities with the purpose of multiplying. If a Home Group reaches a large number (20 people for example), you will lose the essence of small group which is to give satisfaction to each participant through being encouraged to speak freely and to be accepted. That large number doesn't allow people to have an effective discussion about the reading. That will make it difficult to make a Weekly Goal and gain a victory through personal growth.

Concepts of the stages of the multiplication of cells

First stage: a cell reaches the sufficient number of people to multiply through members and the joining of new people (12). When the cell multiplies into two, this is the first stage of the multiplication.

Second stage: Next, each of the two cells repeats the first stage, after reaching the sufficient number of members (12) due to the entry of new members and guests. This is the second stage of the multiplication. From 1 to 2 groups and 2 to 4 groups.

Third stage: After the second stage, when each one of the cells multiplies again, we will have the 3rd stage of multiplication. From 1 to 2 of 2 to 4 and from 4 to 8 groups.

The leader of the original cell should love and care for the cells that are the result of its first stage of multiplication. This does not mean that he conducts the meetings of the two cells; he should give autonomy to the new leader of the cell, but should support him so that he has victory as leader of his own cell. Since the beginning of the formation of the first cell, the Home Group leader must already be preparing a person to be the next leader, for when the cell multiplies. The assistant leader must work together with the Home Group leader to receive training before the multiplication.

Without preparing another leader in advance, there will be difficulties to multiply later.

When multiplication happens, the second stage of the complete multiplication (two to four), the leader of the original cell must continue to take care and love the other three cells that are formed through its multiplication.

The definition of these positions is not exact but one should properly consult with the local central figure.

Limitations of witnessing through the linear system to create a national growth explosion

Until now we have been using a linear system of witnessing (single discussion, without depth) How has the system worked? Members go to a local area and invite a large number of people (1,000 people). Between them, a small portion goes to the church and attends a conference (60 people). Of these, a small part (15 people) participates in a 1 day seminar. And of these, only a percentage goes to the 2-day seminar (6 persons). Later a minimal portion participates in a 7 days seminar (3 persons). After the seminar, perhaps, only a small number among them (2 persons) will be converted to members. That is how the linear system works in a similar way to filtration, survival or "a production line"). From the concept of the number of dimensions, going in one direction or in one dimension only, there is no height or depth. That may be like a hose pipe that has only one input and one output. By placing 1000 on one side, investing energy to send the invited people to seminars; but leaving only two on the other side of the hose. This means that to win 4 we place 2000. This system works, especially to restore people of a high level, however, it has limitations. It only has one input and one output, the system does not allow the desired explosion of witnessing to happen.

With the Home Groups, we can think of a "flat" dimensional structure, where we can increase infinitely the number of Home Groups. This will increase the potential for new members. Each small group becomes a centre of witnessing or a witnessing centre.

The national witnessing explosion will not happen only through an external Home Group system, although it is an excellent system. The explosion occurs as a result of the victories: internal unity, love, victory in the foundation of faith and substance, etc. On the other hand, even though we have internal victory, if we use a system that prevents the explosion, then likewise, national growth will not result. It is possible only through Home Groups, One-to-one Seminars and Oikos (Home Church).

Three points that were important to the victory of Home Groups (multiplication)

Two Home Group leaders gave their testimonies and spoke on the same subject (the same points of victory).

1. 100% Unity of heart with the central figure (pastor or missionary), unity with Abel.
2. Unity of heart between the leader and assistant leader. Unity of Cain.
3. Helping the Home Group members to achieve the "Weekly Goal".

These united leaders succeeded with their Abel figure and their Cain figures, then the three positions made a single body. This is the strongest condition for the victory of the providence.

Points to Note

The Home Group does not receive tithes or contributions; these must be donated only to the church to which it belongs. We can raise money to support activities in the Home Group, for example, buying T-shirts, snacks, etc. By designating one person responsible to administer it, but that is not the same concept of tithing and regular contribution.

One Group has a simple system, the members make a very small donation each week (£1 or €1) into a collecting dish which is used to buy snacks and stationary etc.

The Home Group should not perform Sunday Service and nor should it replace it.

The three points that may cause the Home Group not to be successful:

1. Not following exactly the official guidance for Home Groups.

Although we hear an exact explanation of how to make a Home Group but if we don't follow it, insisting on our own way, we can end up making another kind of Home Group without purpose.

2. Perform only Home Group activities and don't make One-to-one tuition.

Perhaps for a long time, the group has only been holding the meeting, reading, and enjoying fellowship between the same members, without witnessing. And when finally they witness, the guest was sent directly to the seminar without having any link with the Home Group.

3. Not Attending Home Group Visioneering seminars

Due to a lack of understanding, you can end up having only a limited personal understanding that the Home Group is to grow your church more. But without understanding clearly, it is difficult to carry out the Home Group providence. You must always attend the Home Group Visioneering Seminars with maximum participation of members.

Chapter 4.
Testimony of Ms. On-Nan

A testimony given in the Home Groups visioneering seminar, 'One-to-one and Oikos (Home Church)'.

Ms. On-Nam has already given this testimony publicly on several occasions at True Father's request. The lecturer for this seminar requested that she give this testimony because it combines important issues about the application of Principle with one of the essential activities of Home Group, the weekly goal.

"Some people already heard my testimony on other occasions. It is a testimony about how we overcame difficulties after having received the Blessing. Today we have reached a level in which there are virtually no major fights between us as spouses.

In 1990 I went to Russia to do a PhD and there I met our Church. Previously I was a communist and did not believe in God or in the spiritual world. For me, those who believed in God were weak-minded people. But, arriving in Russia, my grandmother began to appear in my dreams. She died when I was three years old and I never met her. But when I described her to my mother, she told me that my grandmother was exactly that way when she was alive. This intrigued me and I started to search for explanations in several religions. I started to visit some evangelical churches. At that time, Russia was opening its borders to other countries (perestroika) and there were quite a few Christian churches from South Korea being established. As I still did not know the Russian language, I was looking for answers in these Korean churches.

I told the pastor there that I would like to have faith in God as they did. He insisted that they would teach me how to have faith. But all the pastors responded in the same way, saying that God is something that if you believe in Him, He exists, but if you don't believe, He does not exist. For a person of communist mentality, that was not a satisfactory answer.

At that time, our Church offered seminars for university professors and they invited me to participate. I listened to the Divine Principle (Creation and Fall) for the first time and I liked it a lot. The same day I became a member. I put many questions to my spiritual father and he gave me all the answers. In the second seminar, already other teachers were invited and I helped as staff. The process to enter the church and accept the Divine Principle was very quick.

After completing a doctorate in Russia, I was invited to teach at Sun Moon University. In 1995, I received the Blessing with my husband, who at that time was studying at UTS in the United States. After graduating UTS, they sent him as one of the 33 missionaries to Jardim, in Brazil. At that time, I was still teaching in Korea. I did not even know what it was like to be a missionary, but I thought that I had to go to help his mission, because he was very shy and could not communicate very well.

I had only one year's experience as a dedicated member and always had good results in witnessing and many testimonies of bringing guests. For this reason, my spiritual father always praised me and told me that I was the best in such activities. I felt proud and perhaps a little arrogant since I was young and already a university teacher (this was not very common in Korea). I did not know about the formula course, I thought only that those external results which made me proud were sufficient for the life of faith. I thought that because of my situation, I was already at a level where I could help my husband in his mission.

I asked for a temporary license from the university to try and come to Brazil, but due to the difficulty of getting the visa, I went first to Uruguay. After that I could go to Brazil and begin family life.

Once, we were giving Holy Wine door-to-door on a sunny day in Campo Grande. Suddenly, my husband said that the sun was very nice, as a red circle, rather like the flag of Japan. When I heard him say "flag of Japan", it gave me a shiver and an image appeared in my mind: there was a large hole and Japanese soldiers were burying Korean men alive. The Koreans tried to flee, but the Japanese kicked them and pushed them into the hole again. I was horrified, cold and sweating. I thought that was because of some film that I might have seen, or something in my head, because I had never had that kind of spiritual experience previously.

Another situation always happened when I was washing clothes. The noise of the washing machine made me distraught, because I saw a lady of more or less 35 years of age with a child strapped to her back and another taking her hand. The noise seemed to me like the sound of Japanese aircraft, dropping bombs on top of this lady who ran desperately from one side to another. I felt panic and only returned to normal after disconnecting the washing machine. I felt very strange, but I did not understand that it was a spiritual experience.

One day I was cutting vegetables for lunch and heard the voice of a man of about forty years old telling me: "take that knife and use it wisely to kill that Japanese, you can't have a Japanese son. Here in Brazil it is as hot as hell, here is not your place, your place is giving classes in the university in Korea, go back over there". I had fought many times with my husband up till then, but never had thought of killing him. For the first time I thought it must be a spiritual experience.

Then, I told all the experiences I had had to my husband and he said that we had to do prayer and conditions for freeing the spirit. I had little faith and did not understand yet what he was talking about. He wondered how many minutes of prayer I was able to do and that wounded my pride. I replied that I could do seven minutes for seven days; that was little to him, but that was the standard of my faith at that time. Then we started the condition.

I prayed saying as well: "I know that you are my ancestor who died during the war against Japan and because of that you have resentment, but now is not a time in which we resolve things through revenge, trying to kill another person. Today there is a better solution than revenge, it is liberation; please accept this idea. My husband also prayed by apologising for my ancestor in the place of his ancestors. He told them he had come to Brazil to establish conditions for restitution on behalf of the ancestors through his dedication to the public mission. I did perceive what that ancestor was feeling. It seemed that he felt unsolved resentment of so many years. I told him that he should trust me, and believe that the merit of the age would be employed and True Parents foundation, Heung Jin Nim and Dae Mo Nim.

On the sixth day of prayer, I felt that this spirit had gone. Then, suddenly I felt the situation improve quite a lot. Before that, over any small matter, we had arguments and finished up feeling resentful, because our ancestors had been enemies.

When my husband spoke Korean, speaking in the Japanese way, it caused misunderstandings between us. When I got sick, he asked me in Korean if everything was fine with me. I felt that it was very strange, if someone sees that you are sick and still asks you if everything is alright. I was very angry because if he could already see that I was ill, why did he wonder if I was OK! But that was actually a misunderstanding of language. That was the way of he expressed his concern and affection, he did not have any bad intention.

Before I felt that there was a great spiritual barrier between us, but after the spirit left, I felt that a hole in this barrier had opened up, and when he said that he loved me, I could feel something deeper than before (due to the difference of the Korean culture). I felt that our relationship as a couple had grown to a higher level and the feelings could flow better between us.

But our fallen natures still remained strong, clashing against one another. At that time, when we went out witnessing, I always went with elegant clothes and garish, high-heeled shoes. When he found a person on the street, even if it was with a heat of 40 degrees, he stood and sat talking for a long time with that person. My makeup began to melt, my clothes started to bother me because of the heat and my feet started to hurt because of the high-heeled shoes. That was the way he was trying to give love to the members, but I was irritated a lot because of that. I thought "Why does he not at least go to a shady place to talk? ". Among Koreans, it is very common that someone could interrupt a discussion and it would not cause any problems, but he would stand patiently listening to the person to finish the whole story. When we got home, we quarrelled because of that.

When I felt this kind of anger I attracted all those feelings of the Korean ancestors again, and when he got angry with me, I also felt as though the Japanese ancestors were treating the Koreans with contempt. So it was not a simple fight between two people going on, but a war between the ancestors of the two sides. When starting a fight, everyone wanted to speak words stronger and tougher than the other.

For several days, in prayer, crying desperately, before sleeping, I said to God: "Heavenly Father, you said this was a blessing, but I feel I am in hell! " I repeated this prayer for many days until I thought God must be bored of hearing the same prayer every day. One day, when I tried to pray with different content, I heard a voice, and to this day I do not know if it was an ancestor or my original mind, telling me: "On-Nan you're an ass! ". I got really scared and thought: "I'm not an ass; I am a university professor with a doctorate. Who says I'm a donkey? But, once again I heard the same voice, like the first. "On-Nan" repeating the same thing, I felt as if two "On-Nans" were discussing inside me, On-Nan "A " against On- Nan "B ". Then, the other On-Nan says: "On-Nan, does it seem easy to you to change your character? At that moment what came to mind was a Korean saying, "With the passage of time the sea and the mountains can change, but the character of a man never changes." There I realized that to change myself was very difficult. Before, my husband had told me about the standard of individual self-improvement, but I did not understand. I thought I did not need to change my nature. When I am angry I can speak angry words; when I'm happy, I can smile my way; if I am hungry, I will eat, and if I need sleep I will sleep. I was unable to distinguish between the desires of the original nature and the desires of fallen nature. That was why he said he had to accept my nature no matter what, because I was the person he had received the blessing with.

The other "On-Nan " said it was for that reason that I was raising hell for myself. I was seeking to change the character of a man. But I did not perceive it that way, I thought my way of doing things was correct and, therefore, my husband had to act the way I wanted. If I was cleaning the house and, if by chance he entered and did not wipe his feet, I had to challenge him; for me, that was correct. When he goes to bathe he must put his dirty clothes in the hamper, if perchance he put them outside the basket I would argue with him, because my way was the right way. I felt it was not fair because I went with him to witness in the street, but when I returned, I needed to do the cooking, ironing, washing, collect the clothes he left anywhere, etc. For me, I was not insisting on my own way of doing things, I was insisting on the right way to do things.

What I had not thought of before was, my husband is a man who has his own character and different thoughts from me. I like to worry about the home, clothing, organization, etc., but he would be more concerned with other things, such as mission, the church, etc. I really wanted to change my husband, to my way of seeing things and my way of thinking about things. I felt that because of that, I was creating my own hell. I understood that I was the one who always tried to fight first, annoying him. I was raising hell for myself and then jumping in there and trying it out again. After quarrelling, we stayed for a few days without speaking. Because of the pride of us both, and that was causing resentment in me. I wanted out of that situation. I was living in hell for many years, but I needed help. Then I got the answer. I needed to do the opposite of what I was doing until then and began to act in ways that he liked and not in my own way. I determined to change and I become the woman my husband expected.

But I did not know where I should start. I did not know what change he would be looking for. First I tried to change my clothes to the way he liked. I liked dark clothes and he liked lighter-coloured clothes. Then the next day I went to buy clothes. Actually I started to realize that I was doing things just the way I liked. I bought my clothes the way I liked and bought him clothes, too, the way I liked.

I never thought to ask if he liked it or not. In those days always I wore short hair, but I started wearing if long, after realizing that he liked that. But he said nothing, not praising me.

After a while, I realized that they were not exactly the things that I needed to change. Thinking the motive of our fighting was never because of clothes, hair, house cleaning, etc. He always insisted that I should love members more, go witnessing, Things that had nothing to do with the house.

He explained to me that the way to solve our problems in marriage horizontally was for each of us to look more to our vertical relationship with God and develop love for Him, through conducting public activities, but for that we had to "forget one another a little ". I had never understood before when he had explained this theory to me, but on that day, I felt that the 'penny dropped'.

He would always wake first for morning HDH and then would wake me up. Sometimes, I did not feel like it and would ask if we could do it at another time, but he insisted and even pulled me out of bed, if necessary he would carry me. After that, I got up but did not want to do HDH because of my hurt pride. That day was beginning badly. As he always pushed me to do HDH, conditions and prayers, I realized that what my husband wanted was a woman of faith with different habits. I should transform to become a woman of faith. I felt it would be very difficult because for a person who did not have much faith until then, it would not be easy to acquire faith suddenly overnight.

When he sent me to make conditions, I always felt that hurt my pride, so, I began to make conditions before he asked me to. Initially that was my motivation, but then I began to experience the real value of making conditions. Before, I only did seven minutes of prayer, but then I determined to do 21 minutes and so on, my ability to pray grew, until I could do five hours of non-stop prayer. Also, I began to increase my ability to do bowing conditions (12, 40, 120, 1200, 3000, and 4000).

Whenever I increased the intensity or amount of my condition, I felt that my spiritual strength to pass any test also increased. Before, due to any small irritation I would have a fight, but later, as my spiritual capacity increased, those small situations, such as leaving clothes out of the hamper, would not cause me any problems. When our faith grows, the level of our acts of devotion must also increase to accompany our faith. If our faith increases to a higher level and we continue doing the same level of indemnity condition, it may stagnate. There is no need to always systematically increase the level of conditions (e.g. increase bows 120, 1200, 12000, or reading, 40 min., 4 hours, 40hrs, etc.). But at least one time you have to break the barrier of the conditions above your own level of faith. For example, at some time break the barrier of 8 hours of prayer, but it does not mean that you have to do 8 hours prayer every day, you can keep the pattern of say, 40 minutes daily. Every time you challenge your own limits of faith; then love, emotion and spiritual capacity increase.

After doing enough conditions, I felt my "spiritual muscle" (spiritual power) increasing and it became easier to overcome tests.

Tests constantly appear in our lives – just actively do something in the Providence and they will appear. When a member is quite determined and dedicated toward God's Providence, Satan will try to do something to discourage him, maybe through an accident, or other things. Satan wants to break the will that those members have to devote to the Providence. The higher the level of our determination, the higher the level of test that appears. These tests prove how much we keep our determination towards God and the Providence

We are midway between God and Satan. Our life on earth is a constant struggle to demonstrate the characteristics of either God or Satan. On one side God insists that we are his children because of blood lineage through the blessing, and on the other, Satan insists that we are his children because our fallen nature exhibits his character. Our attitude here on earth determines which way we go, to God's side or Satan's. The tests appear as a test from God and Satan, to check our attitude. What do our natures show? God and Satan are looking at the attitude a person will adopt. If we fail and demonstrate our fallen nature, it is a condition that Satan will take and God cannot do anything.

If one does not pass a specific type of test, it will always reappear through another person (spouse, children, members, family, etc.), for the purpose of the test is to decide who wins the fight, God or Satan. The tests in school come in the form of a piece of paper marked with date and times, but in the spiritual life tests of faith are not like that. When we reach our limit of love, our physical limit or emotional limit, the tests appear. At such times it is very difficult to overcome, but we know that there are opportunities for us to make the foundation of substance, after a time of making the foundation of faith.

Our spiritual growth happens as if we are climbing the steps of a ladder. Whenever we go to a higher level, tests appear. We can establish the foundation of faith through our daily life of faith, giving tithes, participating in the Sunday Service, etc. After that, to rise to a higher level we will have to overcome tests in the foundation of substance. Someone will test us in a substantial relationship. Normally the tests come with people who are closest to us, spouses, children, friends, etc. If I give up and abandon these efforts, my spiritual growth will be stuck in the same place. Sometimes even one's financial life is related to that spiritual growth.

If one fails in a test the first time, then it will return a second time. Although it is the same type of test, it will come with greater spiritual weight.

After making many indemnity conditions, our relationship improved considerably, but there was a specific issue that caused problems: Although I like cooking, living in Campo Grande was difficult, because with a little son crying in my arms, and with it being very hot, I had to put the baby on the table to finish cooking lunch. After that, I called my husband to eat the meal but he was translating Japanese to Portuguese and did not give any response; he didn't come. This irritated me. I got angry and I went to the office and I fought with him to get him to come and eat. He felt that I was angry and he went very still and ate in silence. At the table I was irritated because he did not speak. If at least he would talk to me and enjoy the food - that would give me some comfort, but it just didn't happen. That was an issue where I repeatedly failed and became irritated.

One day I realized that this was my "weakness " and began a prayer condition and reading for forty minutes to overcome this. In the first weeks of the condition, I was tense and I always remembered my goal was to not get angry when that situation occurred. But in the course of making this condition it became just a routine, and sometimes I missed my goal. This was a situation where the foundation of faith and the elements of the foundation of substance were disconnected.

Then one day the same situation arose again. After the food was ready, I called him but he did not respond and did not appear. Back came an uncontrollable irritation. I went angrily to the office door. I was about to open it, ready to fight, but I remembered that my condition was precisely for overcoming this issue. It was the last week of the condition. In my mind came a thought that repeated several times: "you cannot fail!" So, I faked a smile, opened the door and told him, without showing any anger, "Aren't you hungry?" He saw me and said: "You go as you are happy now; I think I'll continue to work a little more." That irritated me even more and I quietly closed the door and returned to the kitchen. Then I just walked from one side to the other, with my son in my arms.

I absolutely wanted to overcome that situation, I felt angry when I had more influence from spiritual forces and it was almost impossible to control. Obviously I had no reason to be mad, but had no control. Whenever the situation started, I could not bear it and I got angry.

I wanted to do something different from what he had done in that situation. So I made some tea to take to my husband. I was so nervous that when I picked up the cup, my hand was shaking. When I offered him tea, he continued to concentrate on his work in silence. It was as if he was completely ignoring my existence. That once again led me to the limit of my emotion. I could not let him win, so I made more of a challenge for myself, I said, "You must be tired, I'll give you a back rub." I stood behind him and started to massage with great force. When I put my hands on his shoulders, indeed, what I wanted was to strangle him, but of course I didn't do it. I started massaging his back strongly (for I was really angry) and something extraordinary happened that I only experienced once in my life. After I got to the peak level of my effort, from the deepest place in my heart came an unexplained, immense feeling of joy. I saw all that anger I was feeling at the beginning become a great feeling of happiness and unconditional love. Making that massage was the last resort I had to use to overcome the situation. If it had not worked, I would not have known what to do anymore.

The external environment we were in was not very nice. There were cobwebs, the paint was already well-worn and it had old, simple furniture, but at that moment, everything looked very beautiful and happy, because I had experienced an inner change, a growth in heart and love. The atmosphere did not change physically, but everything looked beautiful because of the internal victory.

I saw my husband and he looked very cute. One who a few minutes ago I had been hating as my enemy, at that moment I saw him as a "prince". The "toad" had just become a "prince" in my eyes and I was experiencing such joy mixed with a feeling of gratitude for him as my husband. I felt that this was a taste of the Kingdom of Heaven.

The joy was so intense that no matter what I did, that wonderful feeling continued. Everything and everyone around me seemed to me to be so beautiful and happy.

At that moment I felt the voice of God saying "Is that On-Nan? Congratulations! I always knew you'd beat this, and you won". After that I continued massaging him and that feeling was still present with me. I realized that the decision to live in heaven or in hell is only up to me and does not depend on others.

When I was angry, I always accused him saying that the fault was his, but I now realized that the decision was solely mine. To be in heaven or hell does not depend on the attitude of the other person, but depends on our own attitude, the source is inside each of us. I realized that in the life of faith, we must not fight against people but against oneself. What matters is whether or not we get control or overcome fallen nature within us. Such tests are part of our life of faith and will always come. If we have no such tests we cannot grow and show God that we are truly his children. After I overcame that situation, I felt the relationship between us was much easier and my spiritual strength increased.

I realized that my heart had indeed held some resentment. The words I spoke when I was irritated were based on this resentment that was hindering my spiritual growth. I decided I should remove these feelings if I wanted to continue to grow in the life of faith. I started a 120-day prayer condition to solve that. I literally prayed to God for help. I said, "I know, God, that I have been keeping this same garbage (resentment) inside me, but I do not want to continue this way". I was desperate and cried without caring if people would hear me or not. After 80 days I felt my indemnity condition had cleaned everything. I felt like a new person and completely free. I could control perfectly the excitement in situations where before I would always fight and express resentment to my husband.

As explained in the lectures, we have many bundles of fallen nature to remove. When we fight against and overcome that which is the most difficult (that main or strongest challenge) then removing less troublesome fallen nature will be easier. After I fought and conquered, I felt it was easier to overcome other problems one by one.

Our relationship improved considerably compared to before, but I still wanted to improve. I realized that what disturbed our relationship was pride. Whenever we discussed something, because of pride we were left not talking for a while and the relationship cooled. I felt I had to break that pride. Then I asked him not to pour gasoline on the fire but water. Whenever we discussed, he began to use logic to point my mistakes ("Just now you spoke well, but you're already talking differently, etc.") That irritated me even more because I was not looking for logic, but was expressing my passion. I honestly said I needed his help to overcome this test. He agreed to help. But I explained that when he tried to hug me I might refuse because of my pride, but he should not give up but embrace me more strongly. As my passion went up and down so quickly this was the way he could help me.

At that time we were taking care of dedicated members in our church. There were two things in my life of faith that were difficult to identify and overcome. The first was to see that Satan was inside of me. My husband always explained to me that, being in the position of Abel, if I did not separate from Satan in myself first, I would never get to separate Satan in Cain. I could not understand what he meant. We had a member who always repeated the same mistake several times. I argued that we ought to send one member back home because he did not register as a dedicated member. I was very angry with the situation. My husband told me I had to separate Satan within me. I was more annoyed saying it was not to me he had to say those things and it was not that Satan was in me but that it was the member who was making such mistakes. He then said: "If you do not have Satan within you, then why are you so irritated?"

After that, I thought, "Is what I'm feeling now is a characteristic of God? Could it be that God is like this, judging human beings when they make a mistake?" I sensed it was not like this. This was not the character of God. So if I was not acting according to the way of God, whose nature was I demonstrating? I discovered that when I was angry, I was acting in a satanic way, showing fallen characteristics.

My husband told me it was a test for me, but I did not understand. Then I began to realize that whenever I reached my limit (of emotion, of love, of faith) I became irritated. Only then I did I manage to see that it was a test.

After I was married, I always lived among many full-time members who helped me grow. When the person in the position of central figure is irritated (mixed with their own fallen nature), they should not try to educate an individual, because when done like that you can even kill a person spiritually. That is why when absorbed with anger because of some member I did not speak, but withdrew myself from the situation to be able to cool my mind. But that only served to entertain, and not completely solve my anger. Whenever I found myself with that member, again my anger would rise up. At first, it took about a month to fully resolve such a problem. Then by degrees this time decreased, first three weeks, then two weeks, one week, one day, one minute... in the end, I could control it as it happened.

If someone who is in the position of central figure, even while using the content of the Divine Principle, uses fallen nature to try to educate an individual nature, that member will close the door of their heart and might even leave the church because of that.

After I was determined to control my anger in dealing with members, God showed me another secret: God was using even the fallen nature of that member to educate me, to bring out my fallen nature. When I came to Brazil, I thought that as a missionary I had come to educate and give life to people in the fallen world, but in truth, God was using the Brazilians to educate me. God's first intention was to educate and remove the fallen nature that was within me that I could become His true daughter. When I came to understand this point, I felt that the mission became much easier. I began to overcome the tests more easily. So if any member spoke ill of me or misunderstood me, I was not so concerned about correcting them, but I wanted to understand what God wanted to teach me through this, about my anger, fallen nature, etc. If I had not come to understand that and had only looked at things horizontally, resentment would have arisen within me against that person. We get to see things from the vertical point of view and not just the horizontal. God and Satan are in a game to see whether or not we exhibit fallen nature. When we show our fallen nature, the game comes to an end and Satan wins. If we do not show the fallen nature, the game also comes to an end, but this time it is God who wins and we can go to a higher spiritual level. After that, we rise to a new spiritual level and begin again.

When we get to show gratitude, even in situations where the other is wrong, God brings us to his temple. The temple of God is called "gratitude". When we show our fallen nature, Satan takes us to his temple. The temple of Satan is called "resentment". We decide which temple we enter.

If we do go through such tests often, and win, resentment will build up within us and will hinder our growth. So the first thing we have to do when we discover that we have built up some resentment is to make a strong prayer "fighting the evil spirits and Satan" and asking God to get rid of this "junk" within us. I have the conviction that this works well, as I have already experienced it. This was a point that was very difficult for me to understand in my life of faith.

Even after understanding this, when I can't control my nature properly I get very frustrated with myself and I feel that Satan is accusing me in order to discourage me. Then again I'll wake up and be sorry for fighting because my goal is individual perfection. If we are overly humble, we are leaving our position and if we were arrogant, we are also leaving our proper position. We have to stay in our own proper position."

Chapter 5.
One-to-one Seminars

Concept of witnessing

When we find a guest through witnessing, sometimes the first thing that comes to mind is to send him or her to a seminar. Of course, that is not wrong, but today, we have an option that is more in line with Home Groups and that is to start One-to-one seminars. Although we do not stop the 7 days workshops, the main activity is the One-to-one seminar. Through this method of education, we have the opportunity to have experiences that we would not have if we simply sent the guest directly to a workshop. Within the Home Group, with patience, we must take care of the guests.

When you the spiritual parent, realise that the time is right, you can start the One-to-one seminar. It is not necessary to force it if you do not already have a relationship of trust and friendship, you can always wait a little longer before you begin. First, we must take care of the guest within the Home Group.

For a Home Group to develop correctly, one needs to do One-to-one Seminars with each one of the guests. If no one is doing One-to-one teaching, the Home Group may fail to develop, because the guests will not learn the essence of Divine Principle. Each member of the Home Group must do One-to-one with their guests. The guest reads the red part and the member reads the blue part. Beyond that, you can read the yellow and white parts at any time. You can also expand on the content that you read with further explanations. Through One-to-one, the spiritual parent can lovingly invest in their guest more directly.

Preparation of the material

To study on a One-to-one basis, we should use both the Divine Principle and a coloured 3 hour booklet of the Exposition of the Divine Principle with diagrams or display the diagrams on the computer. We should not break these rules and use other materials. Also we cannot do One-to-one Seminars reading the diagram booklet on its own without using the Divine Principle book. This will delay our witnessing efforts. If we set up a system outside of these rules in our own way, this will inhibit nationwide development.

We can do One-to-one Seminars with several people, but not at the same time. For example, we can make arrangements for each person on different days of the week. There is no need to wait to complete reading the entire Divine Principle with one person before you begin reading with a second person. We can organise sessions with several people, on different days and at different times, maintaining a full schedule.

One-to-one Seminars provides experiences that would not be possible if the guest was sent directly to a 7 day workshop. When the spiritual parent participates in a One-to-one Seminar in a Home Group, they can experience the role of a lecturer giving the word and experience the role of caring for the guests just like staff on a workshop. In this way, the spiritual parent may also grow. All spiritual children have been given birth because someone took care of them from the beginning. Through caring directly throughout the process of growth of one's spiritual child, the parent can also grow, because they will have to overcome their lack of capacity to love many times and break through barriers to love their spiritual child.

It would be ideal to do the One-to-one Seminar within a short period of time (even 3 days, 4 days, a week etc.) if the spiritual parent has time. The reading can be completed in 3 or 4 days if reading for 10 hours per day.

Words of True Father about One-to-one Seminar

On one particular occasion True Father requested an analysis in Japan of how many people can give lectures for the 21 day seminar. After the result, he said:

"Why am I so surprised? I asked for an inquiry into how many people can give 21 days from among the members of Japan and the outcome of the request was 47 people. Then I was just so surprised. This is wrong. It is sin. Once we have more than 30,000 or 50,000 members it is possible to have these 50,000 members study Divine Principle from the book, but yet only 47 people were educating (doing seminars), this is a great sin". (254: Oct 87. 1994)

True Father used the word sin, emphasising his expectation of a very different result. If we had 50 thousand members, 50 thousand people should be giving lectures, but only 47 are in the process of doing so. That is why True Father was very sad.

On 20 July 1994 at a meeting of regional leaders and leaders in Han Nam Dong, True Father gave directions on how to educate with the book. (11,261 . - 257)

"Start reading, the book has all of the content; stick to this content, and don't do it any other way" (True Father)

Another day, True Father, for emphasis, returned to this subject:

"Among all the Japanese members who are Church Leaders or lecturers, we have 47 people who can give 21 day workshops. This is a great sin. The lifebelt that saves the members' lives is to live according to the words. This can't be done in a workshop. You yourself must care for and develop your own life. The Church isn't meant to do that. Then, how can you care for and develop your spiritual life? With the 'Word'. If you believe that those who participated in the 21 or 40 days workshops are members of the Unification Church, this is a great mistake. They have to study centring on the Divine Principle book. During the time of global struggle, while receiving persecution from the federal government, in the midst of this situation the communists made a strategy through an underground organization. Part of this strategy was not to use public meetings or workshops. They studied with books".

"I see the fact that the members of the Unification Church of today created this type of culture as a big mistake, even though they have a profound truth. That is why I have been saying since last year absolutely do not do lectures. It has to be done with the Divine Principle book".

When we heard these words of True Father more than 20 years ago "absolutely do not do lectures", we did not understood it fully. But we can see that the direction has already changed since that time. Before that, True Father himself emphasized the importance of doing traditional workshops and lectures, but afterwards True Father changed this way by giving us the direction to use the book, because it was time for a change.

Rev. Shin Dong Mo has selected 50 pages of Father's words on this matter so that even though True father gave that content in the past, we can hear again today.

True Father said: "Anyone may become a lecturer. When one begins to feel that lecturing Divine Principle is really interesting, one can talk and read to any person in the house. But if you attend lectures, and although you know the content of the lecture, on returning to one's home, you will no longer speak on the same level with a third party".

Although the guest remains excited after the 7day workshop, having understood the Divine Principle and accepted True Parents as the Messiah, usually he will not be able to elaborate the Divine Principle to his parents or friends in the same way that he heard it on the Workshop. They might ask for example: "Can you explain why Reverend Moon is the Messiah?" It is not that he doesn't know the answer. He or she already heard all the workshop content, but, it is not easy to explain in summary form what the lecturer talked about. In this situation he or she will end up saying: "If you were to go to the workshop, you would also understand. Please, participate in the next workshop".

But, there may not be a 7 day workshop at an early enough date. And even when there is a workshop people may not have time available to participate for 7 days. In some cases a bad impression can be given and persist before that they can come to participate in a workshop. But, in the case of a One-to-one seminar, if the people asked for some explanation, at that point we can start a study session with the Divine Principle book. Therein one will find plenty of evidence that True Parents really are the true Messiah.

"If the guest keeps the contents learnt from Divine Principle in their heart, they might at any time in the future use the content they have learned to witness to others in the same way. And in passing on the content to others they will benefit greatly in their understanding of Divine Principle. If one received such a blessed experience or became very excited through the Divine Principle book, we have to pass this content on through the Divine Principle book". (True Father)

According to the principle of "the false precedes the true" we can perceive what God had planned for the future through observing what communism had done. Just as communism has expanded globally, reaching two-thirds of the world, using propaganda books (Marxism) touching the hearts of the people (fallen nature of resentment and anger against the authorities), we, now on the side of God, must use the Divine Principle book to expand our teachings to reach all mankind, appealing to the original heart of people, centring on the true love of God.

Using the Divine Principle book to witness is the clear instruction of True Father. Communism appealed to people's resentment, we must touch the original heart of mankind through the Divine Principle.

Important points that we have to follow with One-to-one Seminar

During the reading sessions, you should not skip any part of the Divine Principle and neither should you change the order of the chapters during the reading. You will not achieve the desired effect if anyone skips some chapters of the Divine Principle and finish too soon. Within the Divine Principle there is enough content to solve all the problems of humanity. We do not know which part of the Divine Principle book has the relevant answer for the life of that guest. There was a case in which the lecturer had wanted to skip the chapter on the Resurrection, but in the end did not skip it. The guest was overwhelmed with exactly this part on the Resurrection, because he had a real life situation that that content could help a lot.

We must not change the structure of the "One-to-one Seminar" (for example, one to two, one to three, one to the whole family...), because to ignore this rule is going to affect the overall reaction over time. If we allow exceptions and change the rules, the percentage of people who become members will be lower.

Sometimes, someone might think that a One-to-one Seminar with the husband and wife together may be faster and more efficient. But this is a great deception. Why can't we make one to two? Between two people, one will become Abel type and another Cain type. Anyone who becomes Cain type may interrupt the other to gain benefit. If it was only One-to-one, the guest can open their heart, gain confidence and begin to describe the difficulties in his personal life and receive personal help, but if you have a third person doing the reading, no one will open their heart and the process to become member will be delayed. Doing this with several people at the same time may seem like a winning strategy, but in truth, you would be losing the chance to offer the condition correctly so that the percentage of positive outcomes after the "explosion of witnessing" would be considerably lower.

There are cases in which the Seminar session is in the guest's house and their family members are in the background full of curiosity. If you can do it in a separate room, that would be ideal, but if not, then continue to maintain the One-to-one Seminar process while the others are looking on. Keep your concentration on the person who is receiving the reading so that only you and she are doing the reading. You should not allow other people to participate in the reading as well, only the spiritual parent and the guest. But there are situations in which people insist on joining in all together. In this case it is good to explain that the method of the One-to-one is most effective and then to agree on a different day or a different schedule for each person. If we explain this with sincerity, love and affection, people will normally accept.

We must not do the One-to-one Seminar with a guest of the opposite sex. In our case, we set up this rule rigidly. The investment of love and emotion over 30 hours between two persons of the opposite sex may cause problems. If you allow exceptions, especially when conversion happens, problems will go on interacting together. Changing these methods and routines and including ideas of one's own will kill off the possibility of national growth.

We must give priority to establishing the correct tradition of the One-to-one Seminar. This is to establish the culture of One-to-one Divine Principle Seminars nationally, preparing as such the basis for future growth nationally. If we accept some exceptions, the powerbase for growth will erode.

Example of a member who experienced victory in witnessing through One-to-one

There is a member in Sao Paulo who works selling vegetables. He got 6 people through friendship with his customers in effect "Oikos (Home Church)" and is teaching them using the One-to-one method. He expressed it like this: "It took 2 and a half months to complete the whole Divine Principle book using the One-to-one method of study with a guest. When I was near the end of the book, the person had almost become member and I received a revelation: After completing the Seminar with 6 persons, encourage them to do One-to-one Seminars with their families and friends, and after you should start to do One-to-one Seminars with 6 new guests ". After this experience, he has continued these activities and has already gained 8 spiritual children.

Growth in the number of Members through One-to-one Seminars.

When a guest concludes the Seminar course (One-to-one) and accepts the Divine Principle, because he is inspired, he wants to pass this content on to other people he knows. If it were up to the traditional lecture method the guest would have to start training as a lecturer, which could take a long period of time as well as waiting for the opportunity of a workshop, but with the One-to-one Seminar method, they can immediately begin the reading of the Divine Principle to more people and thus gain their own spiritual children. This will accelerate the growth and maturity of the guest as a member, because he will have an object of love in whom he can invest. Some real success stories have already happened such as the case of a guest of CARP-Brazil who after going through the reading of the Divine Principle three times, was so inspired that he went looking for a guest and completed the reading of Divine Principle with him, too. Immediately after finishing, that guest was looked after by an older member of the church and now is in the process of becoming a member and starting to do seminars (One-to-one) with a new guest. Yet even though only six months in the church, this person is already gaining her own spiritual children and growing through the process of loving them. She also looks forward to continually participating in a Home Group and other activities of the church.

There is also the case of a person who completed One-to-one Seminars with 15 people. Out of all those, 8 of them became members and among those 8, 6 have begun to do One-to-one Seminars for another 6 people and of those, 2 have already gained their own spiritual children. In this case, in a period of one year, doing witnessing activities with One-to-one, that person has already gained 8 spiritual children and 2 grandchildren.

There are many more cases throughout Brazil in which the members are feeling new hope through applying the One-to-one Seminar method. We must strive to attend God and our spiritual parents in this very important providence. Once we have determined to carry out the will of God, God's blessing will without doubt help us greatly in our activities!

If a member performs One-to-one Divine Principle Seminars for up to 6 persons and has completed within 3 months, following on from that, that member can begin to look for more people to start the seminars (One-to-one) and at the same time, those who have completed have the incentive to begin to do the same with their family members, friends, etc. In this way, after 6 months the member may have gained 18 spiritual children through the One-to-one Seminar method. If many members begin to do the same thing, the growth from witnessing will be accelerated in many places. This would be the ideal way, but we know that in practice it is not as perfect as we would like. It may be that not all those who have completed the Divine Principle reading become members. In addition, those who become members might not want to start doing seminars (One-to-one) immediately. Nevertheless, if some percentage was guaranteed, the result will still certainly be very satisfactory.

Let's imagine that out of a total of 6 people who completed One-to-one, only 3 became members. Of those 3, only 1 starts to get involved in doing one by one with another guest and this guest becomes positive and accepts. At the same time the member is already looking for more than 5 or 6 new people to participate in studying One-to-one. Among these new people, 1 or 2 have accepted and become home members. In this case, although only a small percentage of the guests accepted, after 6 months that member will have 4 spiritual children. Along with that, there will be 5 people who will begin to do seminars (One-to-one) for more guests and thus the numbers will multiply again and again.

Difference between the traditional workshop and the One-to-one seminar.

In a traditional workshop, the probability that the guests become members is at best between 15% and 20%. Through the One-to-one seminar, this possibility increases up to 60% to 70%. Rev. Jong Sung Seo did a survey and concluded that through the One-to-one seminars; approximately 3 out of 5 people become members of the church. True Father has said that a 70% success rate is achievable.

Through conducting One-to-one seminars, the Brazilian church confirm that the result is between 60% and 70%. Let's see below:

Based on the broad experience of witnessing activities, when we saw the result of 60%, we remained a bit concerned, because it is a very high success rate. There were even people who doubted this, convinced that it would only be a one-off result. But, through continuing the research over a period of about a year, we saw that the percentage did not go down. At any time, in any area, the result was always the same with even some states experiencing an even greater result. We want to emphasize that these are the results achieved by the general membership who are not experienced lecturers.

In traditional workshops, it is unlikely that a new lecturer will appear among the participants after the seminar ends. Even after spending so much time lecturing, the lecturer usually has to continue lecturing, because we know that it is not so easy to train a new lecturer. In the One-to-one Seminars, the process to help the guests become members and the process to train them to be a new lecturer occur at the same time. While a spiritual parent is teaching, he/she is also training a new lecturer.

After finishing the One-to-one seminar, the guest will become a new member and a new lecturer. What is the best situation; a few lecturers regularly conducting seminars or all the members teaching the Divine Principle through One-to-one Seminars, and perhaps not knowing how to explain such profound content? If all members in the nation begin to practice this One-to-one method, this will accelerate the process of national restoration much more than just a few teachers giving lectures daily for several people.

With the traditional workshop method, although the guest might want to attend a workshop, he will have to wait until the next one which might be several weeks away. There is also the cost of transport from one place to another.

In a One-to-one Seminar, you can do a Seminar session at any time using the Divine Principle book and there is no workshop fee.

Let's look at a numerical comparison between witnessing with One-to-one Seminars and the workshop method of one to many.

Let's assume that in a nation using workshops, it restores 1000 people per year; after 32 years it will have 32 thousand people, but this is not enough to have national influence.

The same nation, through the method of One-to-one seminars, beginning with one person, using the principle of duplication, even though it starts slowly, by the 15th year it will already have exceeded the other numerically. After passing this point, each year will see a rapid growth in the number of members and after 32 years, ideally it will be 2,147,483,528 people.

If we follow the pattern of restoring 1 person per year, after 32 years we get to 2,147,483,528 people, but, if we continue at the rate of restoring 1 person every 6 months, it will take 16 years and at the rate of 3 months, it will take only 8 years to reach the same result.

But there is something fascinating about this simulation. How can a nation that has the capacity to restore 1000 people per year, only need 1 person to begin giving One-to-one seminars to exceed it by so much? If all the members of this nation began One-to-one, certainly the process of the restoration of this nation would be much faster.

The one-at-a-time method seems too slow to the extent that any real growth can happen. But we need not worry about a goal of 4 million, because this will be the number that will be achieved with the new method. The important thing is establishing the culture that each and every person can do One-to-one in the whole of the country. When this happens, after a short period of time we will find national development will take place.

We need to give continuity to the person witnessed to after concluding the One-to-one seminar

Certainly, after completing the Divine Principle reading the with our guests, we must give on-going education so that they become strong members who deeply understand the Divine Principle, appreciate the traditions of the church and give hope and purpose for their life.

After concluding the seminar (One-to-one) we can send our guests to a 7-day workshop. In the case of sending a guest to the workshop prior to One-to-one, we must have the commitment to do One-to-one seminars with them afterwards. It is not forbidden to do workshops, but we must not do them in such a way as to prevent the deep-rooted culture of One-to-one seminars. One by One is a central providence at this time.

When the central figure is found to be adequate and effective, he may carry out seminars. But the important thing now is in firmly establishing the culture of the One-to-one seminar, until it becomes second nature. Everyone should do One-to-one. After completing it with many people, you will be able to do a workshop in each state with the people who have completed, and in that workshop be able to teach about the life of True Parents, the traditions of the church, internal guidance on the life of faith, etc.

Many people are breaking barriers and doing One-to-one.

After finishing the One-to-one seminar, one should give a diploma and have a small ceremony with the Home Group and guests. They will feel very happy and loved.

How to deal with questions from the guests during One-to-one seminars

It is possible that a guest will ask questions during the One-to-one about the Divine Principle content and the spiritual parent might not be able to provide an appropriate response at the time. In this case one need not lose patience and become nervous or invent an answer just to look good. You can say honestly and sincerely that in the next meeting you will have an answer for them. Then look for the pastor or a missionary to deal with their question, and at the next meeting give the answer. Your sincerity will win over the guest and make them feel good.

You can also request that the guest be patient, because the answer may appear in the following chapters. For example, in a 7-day workshop in the early days, there were always questions asked by the guests, but the lecturer did not respond because he knew from experience that the answer would come up in the lectures in the following days. Coming to the final day of the workshop, when asking if anyone wants to ask a question, usually the answer is no, since they have all been answered in the course of the workshop. In the case of One-to-one, it is the same thing. We can ask that the guest write down their question because the answer will appear in the following chapters.

Sometimes we feel it is difficult to get guests to come or even that we can relate to guests, but maybe they can't do One-to-one due to a lack of time or something else. In such cases we can begin with prayer. God will prepare the circumstances. Some people have experienced this situation when they begin to pray. The guests were invited and those who did not have time, found time and the One-to-one seminar could take place.

There are cases in which the guest does not want to do One-to-one with the whole Divine Principle book, because he feels that it takes too much time. However, when he does the first reading on the first day, he finds it very interesting and the same person wants to continue and the One-to-one until the end.

Testimonies from people who have broken through barriers doing One-to-one.

Some people may feel some kind of barrier to begin giving One-to-one seminars. Nevertheless, what we should do is simply keep going and the barrier will be broken. The One-to-one Divine Principle seminar barrier can seem like a tough nut to crack, and from a distance seems too hard, but if you keep hitting it softly it will break. Let's look at some testimonials from members who managed to break the barriers and achieve good results in their witnessing through One-to-one seminars:

Madam Renilda Rodrigues do Vale Vidotti (Missionary in Itapecirica da Serra -SP):

In the beginning, I was very insecure and afraid of not being able to do the One-to-one seminar. I always thought: If someone asks me questions and I don't know how to respond, what am I going to do? After finding strong determination, I figured out that I would begin with much love, mainly because it is an activity that Heavenly Father is asking for at this time. Then I had my first encounter with a friend and it was a wonderful experience; I felt that God really was with me. Today I actually feel like a bird with wings wide open and without any fear of flying. Currently I'm doing the One-to-one seminar with 4 people and it has been very rewarding for me to serve God and True Parents at this very important time.

Madam Regina Duarte (Home Group leader):

I always thought that I couldn't do One-to-one seminars because I wasn't a lecturer. But hearing about the importance of it and the results achieved, I broke through the barriers and I began to do it with my sister-in-law. I just read the red part and she read the blue and many times when I explained some point, by and by the confirmation of what I had explained would come. And so each time I obtained more confidence, asking God and True Parents to inspire me and also I am already in contact with another person in order to start it with her. I feel sincerely that all the members of Brazil should be really determined and start to do the seminar (One-to-one) on behalf of our True Father of Heaven, Earth and Humanity.

Madam Maria Teresa Padilla (Missionary and Home Group leader in Frank-SP):

In the beginning I felt some difficulty, but my guest was very focused and always maintained an attitude of respect for the Divine Principle. She understood every chapter that we looked at very well. She had understood the part about providential families, where it shows that God always works with a person on earth in each era. When we completed the Divine Principle book, she asked me some questions, for example: How do I participate in the providence in this era? Who is the person that God is working with on the earth at this time? After this, there was a workshop revealing who were True Parents and she accepted fully. Already she wants to prepare for the Blessing and to liberate her ancestors. She has a 16-year-old son to whom she began to witness in order to send him to CARP. Afterwards, she said that from the beginning of reading Divine Principle, she already felt that these words were words of Truth and that she should listen humbly. She also said that it's such an intense feeling not being able to be with True Parents physically, but hopes to be able to meet True Mother someday.

As we see above, many people are breaking through the barriers. Some members are relating that they experienced the love of God when practicing One-to-one with their own children. In another case, a member (for many years) thought that he would never restore his own relatives through One-to-one, but he broke the Tribal Messiah barrier and his family accepted the Divine Principle and became members.

One-to-one Divine Principle Seminars for religious leaders

In some neighbourhoods in Brazil, the members are breaking barriers and starting to do One-to-one seminars with authority figures such as teachers, counsellors, etc., and also religious leaders. Although a person may have a high position in society, she too will be struggling with the common problems of life, such as, education of their children, relationships etc. Through the One-to-one seminar, the Divine Principle reaches all levels of society. People of high or low positions, it doesn't matter, are in need of God and of the Divine Principle in their lives. We must further expand the One-to-one seminars to people in authority and religious leaders too, because these people have the position to influence and guide many people.

Important points when doing One-to-one seminars

1. To carry out the One-to-one seminars is True Father's instruction. Witnessing person to person, one at a time. You must use the One-to-one strategy. All of us need to do this. (PV. Vol. 96-316)
2. Giving One-to-one seminars, we can experience the spiritual power of the Divine Principle in the life of the guest and the spiritual parent alike.
3. To achieve a result of between 60% and 70% is a realistic expectation, when we do our witnessing with the Divine Principle book.
4. Concluding the One-to-one seminar, both the spiritual parent and the spiritual child can give lectures using the Divine Principle book and this speeds-up the process of fulfilling our witnessing goals.
5. The Home Group is an incubator. Although the Home Group becomes a "nest of love", if we are not practicing One-to-one, it will not lead to national growth. It is very important that we combine Home Groups and One-to-one Divine Principle seminars.

Chapter 6.
Oikos (Home Church)

Meaning of Oikos (Home Church)

In Brazil, the Church is using the term "Oikos" to describe their outreach method. The nearest equivalent and perhaps more fitting to Europe is "Homechurch" and applied in a very broad sense, not restricted to the 360 homes concept but expanded to into the wider community in which we live. For the sake of clarity, in Europe we are using the term "Oikos (Home Church)".

Oikos is a Greek word that means *house and the people living in it (including relatives, employees, visitors, a broad sense of the extended family).* Oikos Witnessing (Home Church) is simply relationship-oriented to your life-style, where you spread the word of God in a natural way through several relationship networks that are scattered like a spider's web, it includes persons such as the family, relatives, neighbours, friends, colleagues, partners of the club, etc. ,

Oikos (Home Church) is about testifying to those people who we already know, that we live with every day, such as our neighbours, relatives, friends, etc. First, we start serving them, then with increasing confidence and friendship, after including them in a Home Group and when it is most appropriate, we start a One-to-one seminar. Thus, witnessing is done in a natural way and the people don't reject us. If we do it the opposite way, simply by inviting them directly to a workshop, people may reject us many times and we might even lose their friendship. First, we must make friends so that we have the confidence of the people, before we can be their spiritual parent.

Previously, due to the time of indemnity, we had to cut our relations with the outside world; we had virtually no social life. But, now it is the opposite, we should increase and strengthen relations with the people of the society more and more, because this is a unique time for us and we must become Tribal Messiahs. My life of faith must be connected with my social life. This is the way of Oikos witnessing (Home Church).

First we must establish good relationships to come closer to the hearts of people

In our daily life in society, our character and personality of course bear witness to the people. Now the time is different from the era in the desert. To become Tribal Messiahs we should not separate our life of faith from our social life. Prior to coming to our current situation in time, the members needed to separate from the secular world in order to protect themselves, now with the move into the new providential era, we must go to the society to become Tribal Messiahs. The area of my life of faith must be connected with my social life. So it is possible develop in all areas of society then witnessing can be done in an easier and more natural way. If we separate from society, the work of witnessing will be much more difficult.

We have used various methods in order to attract people to us so we might witness to them, for example, English classes, crafts, cultural events etc. We gathered people who had an interest in that activity and made friends, then we invited them to attend seminars. We call this type of activity to attract people "entry". It is an entry to our witness testimony. But when we opened an "entry", the rest is "a wall". This means that only those who have an interest in that particular activity, for example, English classes, will be able to enter, the others, the majority, won't come. Always the "wall" is greater than the "entry". We can open more "Entry points or doorways", for example, Spanish classes, German classes, Japanese, etc., even so, the "wall" is still greater. People who do not have interest in learning a language, for example, won't want to come.

In Oikos (Home Church), we attract people by showing our experience. In the case of Oikos (Home Church), there is no "entry". There is no concept of "entering through something". There is no "entry" because there is no "wall". Imagine a situation where 360 degrees all around me in which there is no wall. As soon as we use something like an "entry" to the witness, for example, leaflets, language classes, we are not showing our real selves or our life from the beginning. In the case of Oikos (Home Church), from the start, we demonstrate our day to day experience. We must show our practice of love by serving others and living for others.

When we are not doing Oikos (Home Church) and we depend on only a few "entry" points, for example, language lessons, a video centre, pamphlets, etc., it may become difficult to witness, since near our house we may not have these "inputs". But if we are dedicated to making Oikos (Home Church), the number of members locally shall be the number "Entry" points. The number of members shall be the number of "Video centres", the number of Oikos (Home Churches), which are open to 360 degrees, will be the number of "churches". Also, Oikos (Home Church) is a huge opening to enable the "national explosion" of witnessing to happen. When we do One-to-one seminars, the number of members and the number of Divine Principle books will be the number of "seminars".

Despite the fact that we do Home Groups and One-to-one seminars continuously, if it is not on the foundation of Oikos (Home Church), the witnessing explosion will not happen. For this to happen we cannot use a closed system but we must be open 360 degrees around. People may enter from all sides.

When we witness only to strangers, without the concept of Oikos (Home Church), we can easily abandon them if they do not accept our testimony. However, Oikos (Home Church) is different, because our guests are our families, relatives, neighbours, and close friends. They are those with whom we live every day. Even if we experience that witnessing has not given us the result we had hoped for, even so, we have to continue living together with guests and potential guests from day to day. From this point of view, Oikos witnessing (Home Church) has a higher status, since it is more challenging and increases our capacity to invest love, care, and overcome barriers to win over people during our daily activity. This is a lifestyle where our life of faith and our social life are one.

When we live far away from people, and we meet only once in a while, usually we manage to keep control of our character, education and love, but when we have to live together, little by little our fallen nature starts to appear. That makes us uncomfortable and makes it more difficult to love them, because we also have fallen nature.

The difficulty in witnessing is not because of the method we use, for example, the video centre, pamphlets, lectures, reading One-to-one, etc. What really becomes challenging is the part of ourselves that we have to overcome in front of other people. Whether or not we use any form of "gateway" to attract guests, eventually we will have to gain an internal victory over our invited guest by daily love and sacrifice. In the case of Oikos (Home Church), from the very beginning we invest to gain an internal victory with our guest through our daily activity. When we overcome in Oikos (Home Church), our perception of witnessing will not be dependent on an external witnessing system. We will become people who can overcome in witnessing regardless of the external situation. Also, concepts such as "I don't have time, so I can't go witnessing" – these will disappear.

The best example is True Father

The best example is True Father in Hung Nam prison. He won over the prisoners in the beginning without using words, only by his lifestyle. He worked hard and sacrificed himself for the prisoners. All that time he could not reveal that he was the Messiah, he served them just as God serves his children. Before True Father was able to witness, each prisoner felt the love of God through the experience of living with him. The prisoners could feel God in the middle of a hell-like situation, and they couldn't forget True Father. The tradition of True Father is "with the heart of the father in the shoes of a servant". God is the father who is desperately seeking his lost children. If we inherit this same heart, our witnessing will be easier.

If we were to emulate 10% or perhaps only 1% of True Father's standard of practice, we would already be able to win over any person around. We must inherit Father's heart and Father's way of witnessing and determine to invest in Oikos witnessing (Home Church). This is what it means to become a Tribal Messiah.

By encouraging the way of Oikos witnessing (Home Church) we are not denying other forms of witnessing, for example, language classes, crafts, etc., certainly among us there must be a person who joined the church through one of these methods, then they are all good and can work well. In spite of doing some "entry" activities to attract people, we must still invest in the way of Oikos witnessing (Home Church).

The difference between Oikos (Home Church) and the Linear System

When we only have the model of a "linear system" for witnessing what comes to mind is a "production line". The guest goes through each stage in turn ("Entry" > an event at church > one day seminar > an event > 2 day seminar > 4 day seminar > 7 day seminar > member). It is not a bad or wrong method, but it has some disadvantages. If the system were overly dependent on "professional" skills, one person might only be able to support part of the process, for example, one person just does part of "bringing people to an event" another only does the "distribution of leaflets" on the street, etc. In this case, despite witnessing for many years, we would only be trained in one thing and have no ability to develop the other stages, e.g. to act as workshop staff, caring for and personally meeting the guests, etc.

When we implement Oikos witnessing (Home Church), Home Groups and One-to-one seminars, we can invest in and train in all the stages of the process, because we give One-to-one seminars, we take care of the guests in the Home Group, etc.

Parents do not naturally make a "production line" system in the care of children, for example, one person only investing in the role of the mom; another only investing in the nappy changing part, etc. Parental care is integral and in every sense accompanies the whole process of development of the children.

Through the Home Groups, One-to-one seminars and Oikos (Home Church), each one of us can increase the ability to witness and testify.

Our life of faith and our social life should not be disconnected

Within society, we have quite a few relationships and opportunities to witness. According to one survey, it was discovered that we live with a minimum of 100 people every day. These people are for example, our parents, siblings, family members, relatives, brothers, uncles, nephews, close neighbours, people we know in the local area, people who frequent the same places that we do, people at the neighbourhood shops, new neighbours, the parents of our children's friends, employees, pizza deliverers, newspaper and magazine deliverers, etc., neighbourhood leaders, social workers, people that leave the church, colleagues at work and others – the list goes on and on. If we were not focused on the Oikos (Home Church) method, we might feel that there are no people to witness to. This happens when disconnect our life of faith from our social life.

When my life of faith is disconnected from my social life, I might think that within the company where I work there is no opportunity to testify; when returning home on the bus, I think of it as merely transport and not for witnessing; when going to the supermarket, I do not consider the person on the cash register could be a witnessing guest despite meeting them every day. When I decide to go witnessing, the first thought that comes to mind is to grab the church pamphlets and distribute them from door to door. But as we shall see later, the result of this kind of witnessing will only be 3% at best.

A change of mentality needs to happen. Oikos (Home Church) is already a Tribal Messiah activity. Oikos (Home Church) is about looking for witnessing guests from within those people that we have regular contact with. No one needs to lose patience or despair and run away from anyone. Just patiently increase the depth of relationship with people and deepen your confidence with many people. For example, the parents of my son's a friend were invited to a birthday party at his house. We could not miss this opportunity. We felt we needed to go and of course deepen our friendship unconditionally. This is how to testify through Oikos (Home Church). If people perceive that I am trying to be friends only with the intention of witnessing, they will think that I am being selfish. We need to invest and increase friendship by loving unconditionally and living for others.

At the right time, when you feel that the guest can accept freely, then make the invitation to the One-to-one Seminar or Home Group. Before you can be a spiritual parent, you should become friends and have the confidence of the guests. Problems only occur when we want immediate results in witnessing and omit this stage.

The reason why people join the Church.

According to a survey conducted by a Christian church (source unknown), 80% of the people who came to church were first attracted because of a relationship with someone who was already coming that is, through friendship and trust. Around 10% came by themselves, 5% were through literature such as letters and invitations, 3% through professional evangelism and 2%, for other reasons.

Where should I begin witnessing?

When we want to witness to someone, first we have to start by making a good impression before inviting them for any activity. By deepening our friendship and growing trust unconditionally with a few people, some will become very positive. After involving those people in a Home Group, our confidence will increase and deepen even further. Later, at the right time, we can start One-to-one seminars, increasing their respect for us and, finally, accepting us as spiritual parents. Then we can send them to workshops, church events, UPF activities and other related Unificationist organisations. Guests must be guided to receive the blessing and be tribal messiahs. So, where do we begin witnessing? We must begin through Oikos (Home Church).

When we find ourselves in a position to serve guests, the results won't appear quickly. Before serving someone, we must establish a good trusting relationship. If for example, I started to serve as soon as I entered someone's house and began to clean, that person would probably get angry thinking that I don't believe she knows how to clean their own house. We cannot skip the process. First we grow a person's confidence and friendship, and then the spiritual world will prepare the best opportunity to serve that person with exactly what she needs.

Witnessing to a person who does not want to receive anything (understanding the Step by Step Process of Restoration)

1. Being treated as a servant of servants (denial of self)

When a guest rejects words of advice, love and salvation, he ignores the existence of his spiritual parent. This is the stage at which the guest denies everything (and does not accept that the spiritual parent serves him directly). The spiritual parent in unable to establish a witnessing relationship with the guest. During this period, you can make a good condition through investing your love, not changing your attitude and by overcoming the pain of denying the self. If the guest is negative and the spiritual parent cannot serve directly, there is no problem. If you invest love without giving up on your guest, after a period of time, the situation will change, so you can move forward to the next step. If you feel gratitude in spite of the fact that your heart is hurt because the guest rejected your love, you can transform that into an indemnity condition. What is going to decide victory or failure is not if the guest is positive or negative, but if the spiritual parent, without changing his attitude and overcoming the pain of denying himself, can transform the heartache resulting from rejected love into an indemnity condition.

Many people might give up witnessing during this time because they don't understand what is happening. In reality, there is only a limited time period needed to pass through this level. If the person knows what is happening, she will not lose patience and will not despair, and with continued dedication, she knows what will happen after breaking through the barrier at each level.

2. Being treated as a servant

At this stage, you should be more interested in results than in personal relationships. On the foundation of the previous level, an opportunity will arise to serve the guest. At this time, you must somehow find a way, to serve the guest in any way that they need. This is a period in which you should serve him happily by getting some type of result (or solution to a difficulty) before establishing a good relationship of trust. Through satisfying the "needs" of the guest, the relationship of heart will be increasingly deep.

At this time, do not lose patience but be willing to serve him directly. Talking and listening carefully, the spiritual parent can understand the main need of his life and the main cause of suffering in the life of the guest. For some guests it might be, for example, concern about separating from his partner, difficulty with the children, the pursuit of happiness, true friendship, etc., once you serve this need, by helping him, that will turn into love from the guest. Sometimes the spiritual parent has to sacrifice himself to attend to the needs of the guest.

For example, a guest asked to borrow the spiritual parent's car urgently, but this spiritual parent is very careful with his car and he didn't like to lend it. If, at such a time as this, you don't realize that this is an opportunity planned by God to serve your guest, you could miss this opportunity and fail to move forward in the process of witnessing.

Prayer will shorten the time needed by guest. Prayer also allows the spiritual parent to understand the work and intent of God in the background for the benefit of the guest. The focus of witnessing in this period is to serve the needs of the guest. This translates into the love of God that the guest can feel, since your actions were carried out in accordance with the will of God.

By repeating that process regularly, you will pass the level of servant and will go into the level of an adopted child and invited guests will have more interest and a closer heart.

3. Being treated as an adopted child

Trust and responsibility - on that basis, you will receive more trust and be able to open the heart of a guest even more. At this time, the relationship becomes deeper and you can give instructions to the guest because you are more involved in that person's life.

By repeating that regularly, you will pass this level of an adopted child and will go to the level of a child.

4. Being treated as a son: with heart

This is the level where you can experience unity of heart. When you start to feel the heart of a parent, the emotional positions change. Completing the process of natural subjugation, the indemnity disappears from the relationship between Cain (guest) and Abel (spiritual parent).

Then, continuing to invest, you rise to the position of father or mother. There is a reversal of the spiritual positions and you become a spiritual father.

We have to do every part of the process, without skipping any level. If not, we will feel that we do not have any suitable guest to witness to. If you are aware that in the process of witnessing these steps (levels) will occur, you won't give up on your guest despite the fact that he is negative at the beginning. Investing in prayer, we can accelerate this process because of the support of the spiritual world. Opportunities to win at each level will appear more quickly.

Opportunities to overcome heartache at the level of "servant of servants". This is, to love the guest in the form of forgiveness and overcoming heartache.

Opportunities to satisfy to some "need" of the guest at the level of "servant". This is, to love the guest in the form of service.

Opportunity to increase the degree of trust at the level of "adoptive son". This is investment of love for the restoration of the parent's heart.

Overcoming these stages through true love, we will arrive at the level of parents and we will become "spiritual parents", in the real sense. This is with a heart of parents, entering in an atmosphere free of indemnity between Cain (spiritual child) and Abel (spiritual parent).

Oikos (Home Church), Home Groups and One-to-one

Through Oikos (Home Church), we guide the guests towards a Home Group. When we engage in any activity in society, for example, football, tennis, crafts, etc., we have the opportunity to meet with people and do Oikos (Home Church). We shouldn't lose patience and invite the guest to a workshop or to a Home Group very quickly, we should proceed step by step, serving and living for the sake of others. That will naturally advance the process of witnessing to them. At the beginning we only invest in friendship and deepening our relationship. Little by little the guest begins to take an interest, then we can connect them to the Home Group and to One-to-one. Investing in any external social activity is not waste of time, but it is an opportunity to find guests through Oikos (Home Church).

We must serve and love our guests. When we do this, they become friends, and then we deepen the friendship and increase trust and respect. At some point, the guests will feel that we are different people and will tell you about the difficulties of their lives, trusting and opening their heart. This is the process of naturally winning over guests. Performing Oikos (Home Church), we can complete the greater part of that process. After that, it will be easier to invite them to the Home Group in a natural way.

In the Home Group, we need not lose patience and give them the Truth directly. First, we discuss the reading and the "Weekly Goal" and discover what the guest "needs" in his life. As we serve, consoling, supporting, praising, encouraging, and finally, loving him, we help him gain a victory in his life. When the guest experiences growth and improvement in his life to achieve the "Weekly Goal", he will become a happier person than before. After that, we will be able to explain that in the Home Group we use only a part of the Divine Principle to help improve our life, but, if he wants to, he can read the entire book which is full of solutions to several problems and issues in life. He will be very interested and we can begin with the One-to-one Seminar. This way is much better than simply telling the guest that we have the truth, and that he must learn it.

When we have love for our guest, we can realize more clearly what he "needs" in his life. If we really care for the life of the guest, God will reveal the main "need" that he has, in addition to that, you will create an opportunity to help them in their lives.

Appendix 1

The 12 Important Points for the Success of My Home Group

The Home Group Leader should meet with the members once a month and check these points to see where to invest to develop the Home Group.

These points were important for the Home Group to gain success.

1. Does my Home Group maintain a weekly meeting?

2. Are my Home Group members setting, understanding and accomplishing the Weekly Goal?

3. Does my Home Group create a harmonious environment where God can be present?

4. Does my Home Group include new people?

5. Does my Home Group keep focussed on the guests (cares, loves, listens, praises, etc.)?

6. Does my Home Group have a goal for multiplication (e.g. 3, 4, 6 months ...)?

7. Does my Home Group have an Assistant Leader in training to be the leader of the next cell when you multiply?

8. Does my Home Group maintain the features of "a small group"? (Home Group with a small number of people that allows everyone to express themselves, be accepted and interact freely).

9. Can everyone in my Home Group speak and be freely accepted without correcting or trying to change each other?

10. Do all of the members of my Home Group pray for each other and for the success of the Home Group?

11. In my Home Group are we doing One-to-one Seminars with the guests?

12. Does my Home Group giving report of activities, with photos and testimonials, every month?

13. Are the Home Group members reaching out through Oikos (Home Church)?

Appendix 2
Examples of Ice Breakers

1. If you could save just one (or more) memory to take with you to the spirit world (in life after death), what memory (-ies) would you want to save?

2. What has been the happiest moment of your life?

3. What was the greatest compliment you received in your life so far?

4. Let's talk about your closest friend.

5. In what place do you feel most welcome and safe, like being a child again?

6. If you could go back into the past with a time machine, to what time and where would you want to go?

7. When did you feel you did something really satisfying?

8. What are the most beautiful memories with your mom and dad as a child?

9. If you could be a Biblical figure, who would you like to be?

10. Among the 66 books of the Bible, which do you like best?

11. If you could go anywhere in the world, where would you like to go?

12. What is your favourite movie or TV show?

13. Who is the person who has had the most influence in your life so far? (Not including True Father or Jesus or Buddha etc.)

14. What was the best thing that happened last week?

15. What time in the day do you like best?

16. What was the most important thing that happened last week?

17. Where would you like to travel if you could go anywhere in the world for three days?

18. If you could choose a place to live, anywhere in the world, what place would you choose? Why?

19. If there is something that you feel is helping in this meeting, what is it? (Spiritual, emotional, internal, present, etc.)

20. What is your goal in life from now on?

21. If you could have an experience or understanding of the past again, which event would you like to repeat?

22. If you could be the leader of a nation, what country would you lead and why ?

23. If you could talk to any person currently alive, with whom would you want to talk? Why?

24. Assuming you won £50,000.00 in the lottery, please; tell how you would use this money.

25. In which period (historical period) would like to live? And why?

26. Please discuss three reasons that you are grateful to your family.

27. What book, movie or video do you recommend? And why?

28. Is there anything that you have done until now, that you feel gave joy to God? What was it?

29. Where do you spend most of your free time when on holiday?

30. What style of film or music you like most?

Notes

Notes